CEDAR CREST COLLEGE

D1233324

Don Giovanni. ACT II, Scene 1.
(Glyndebourne)

MOZART ON THE STAGE

By
CHRISTOPHER BENN

With an Introduction by
RICHARD CAPELL

and Illustrations by
KENNETH GREEN

780.92

M93zbe

ERNEST BENN LIMITED

LONDON

First Published in September, 1946
Second Impression, March, 1947

The publishers are much indebted to Professor Edward J.
Dent for reading the manuscript of this book, and to the
proprietors of the Music Review for the use of the chapter
on Don Giovanni, which first appeared in its pages. The
drawing of "The Countess" (Le Nozze di Figaro) is reproduced by kind permission of Sir Eustace Pulbrook.

Printed in Great Britain by
Hazell, Watson & Viney, Ltd., London and Aylesbury

CONTENTS

3

34142

ILLUSTRATIONS

INTRODUCTION

ON autumn afternoons in 1941 Christopher Benn and I would bathe in the day at Bagûsh—then Eighth Army headquarters—and stroll between the dunes. Perfect, that bathing beach, the best in all the Mediterranean. And not wholly dead the landscape; a palm-tree or two sprouted in the dip between the seaward dunes and the interminable desert. Migrating birds from Europe came down there for respite, so weary that they could hardly bring themselves to shuffle away from our feet, before they pursued their way to the far south.

Those days were an interlude. The November battle was coming, the Crusader campaign, so called, which Benn was not to see out. It brought back an old time to me, but to him, half my age, it was new—the hopes, the tension, the qualms of the days before battle. The air seemed heavy. Or the fading summer would be threatened by a sharp hint, with wind and breakers in the bay, of the Libyan winter that was at hand.

Of what did we not talk? Benn was serene of temper and shrewd in argument; he was confident that all things did not work together for ill. He seemed to be not so young. It was the eve of battle; and youth is of any age when the morrow may bring eternity. He had seen the end of an era. I had seen two such endings, but one was enough for experience. We talked, for instance, of the chances in the after-war world of the end of men's crow-like blackcoated-ness and the possibility of suits of many colours. Benn, I seem to remember, thought something was still to be said for the top hat. Gingerly we talked of 1940. Will not

all who lived that year talk of it always with a certain ginger-
liness?   Piety or awe requires that certain experiences of
life, love and death, and a remission from death awful
almost as death itself, should not be too insistently talked
about.

There was still no knowing we were not in for another
ice-age.   Then let us—it might be breathing an air cloudy
with sand blown from the south-west—make the most of
our old unclouded days!   Benn, and it is surely a consolation to be dwelt upon, had had these generously allowed
him.   Bright among the hours recalled were Beecham concerts and summer afternoons at Glyndebourne.   We peered
into them fondly as at a peepshow of another world.

I could take a longer view into the era before the other
deluge, and the lucidity came back of my sense, in August
1914, of a world's passing, of a curtain irrevocably fallen
and lights put out.   He would chaff me a little for idealiz-
ing the extinguished splendour, Edwardian Covent Garden,
the first apparition of the Russian dancers, never afterwards
matched in their original quality of a sort of nobleness in
luxury and magical accomplishment, and Chaliapin nights
at Drury Lane, when Chaliapin had not become a wander-
ing prodigy but was a star in a constellation.   Benn knew
the material of all this well enough, and inclined to think
of it as rather tawdry; and I would maintain the poetry
there had been in the incomparable glitter of it all, the
dazzling talents, the princely profusion.   He would argue
that his own experience had been a match; that princeliness
had survived the old war—that there had been princes
between the wars, the Courtaulds and John Christie; that
his youth as well as mine had been the age of Beecham;
that Toscanini's public had little to envy Nikisch's; that
there had been Rosenkavaliers as sumptuous since 1919 as

8

before 1914; above all, that his age, superior to the spell of
ephemeral showiness, had, as Edwardian youth had hardly
done, recognized eternal verities. Of Bach, his sublime
order and ageless authority; and of Mozart, his supernatural
creativeness, rich as Nature's own, but supernatural in the
effect of achieved purpose made by his infallible formal
control.

Benn[1] was a young Englishman of the generation, the
first for centuries, in whose education and culture music was
a regularly planted feature, not a snipped buttonhole, but
a rooted growth. Not an exotic fit for only an exceptional
plot, but proper to the garden of every educated mind. A
chapter of English social history would be wanted to account
for the old frivolity of our appreciation of music and the
consequent impoverishment of the English eighteenth and
nineteenth centuries, the centuries when the European intellect outdid in music the exploitation of all the other arts.
It would be interesting to go into the obtuseness in our
academies to the intellectual claims of music. By what
accident was Greek prosody, through generation after
generation, established as a fundamental study and dis-
cipline for the English governing classes, and the very rudi-
ments of music, the merest musical literacy, ignored? The
judicial humorist who still in the twentieth century can,
in a court of law, raise a laugh by asking for an interpretation of the word "arpeggio," is a product of that deliberate
illiteracy.

I think of Christopher Benn as illustrating the change in
the English intellectual scene worked in this century by
the new class of music-masters in the principal schools. His
musical aptitude was not highly exceptional, and at an
earlier time he would probably have accepted deprivation

[1] 1912–1941.

from music cheerfully enough. But in his day the English schoolboy no longer had to steal his way to music. The door was open, the chance offered him, to be made much of or little; the introduction was afforded him to Bach and Beethoven as to other generations of schoolboys the introduction to Plato and the classic poets.

It came about, this enrichment of the average educated Englishman's life, under the pressure of the phenomenon and the prestige, unexampled in any other civilization, of modern European music. It was more or less inevitable. If Attic tragedy represented the very sublimity of the working of man's mind, not less so did the classical symphony; nor could it, in the long run, be regarded as an inferior study. What can be fairly said is that the English academic acknowledgment, slow in coming, was, when it came, not perfunctory or drily scholastic. The schools may not all have been abreast, but it is the common testimony of English youth that music was made a stimulating subject. The seeming impossible would be undertaken—the execution, for instance, of Bach's Mass—and such an experience could only put a stamp for life on any boy of average susceptibility. The music masters of the principal English schools were in a considerable proportion pupils of Parry, Parratt and Stanford, and the boys they taught inherited a tradition and a standard.

To talk about music with Christopher Benn was often to think of him, with his lively if not all-absorbing interest in music, and his superior intelligence, as an illustrative case, and to start wondering what English musical life might have been if something like Parry's educational influence had begun a century or so sooner. It was tempting to think of him as typical, especially in his devotion to Mozart. Not that he was typically exclusive, after the fashion of

his generation. He would even defend Mahler, whom he
thought a composer underrated in England. But Romanticism and especially Late Romanticism had lost most of
their magic for the generation that was young between the
wars. Not that that was its plight—it was natural; Tenny-
son, too, and Swinburne were in eclipse. The plight of the
generation was remarkably new. This youth was, as no
other generation had been, dissatisfied with its contemporary music. Amused—that was the word in vogue—it
may have been with the dry harlequinade of Stravinsky and
Hindemith, but profoundly dissatisfied. The plight of the
generation was that, with all its new knowledgeableness, it
found itself at the end of an era of European music. The
wonderful summer was over, the harvest garnered, and the
sounds of the air were the crackle of wintry thorns.

The book of the time was Spengler's *Decline of the
West*. Only the scientists and engineers were in a position
to ignore or disallow its confession of lost confidence, lost
faith. The general plight of youth, desperate for a faith of
some kind, was illustrated by the resort of so many generous
spirits to the wastes of Marxian materialism. How barren
was this and hollow was shown up by the absence of its
expression, in any measure worth mentioning, in any of the
arts. Not that anti-Marxianism did any better, if we
except Roy Campbell's *Toledo* poems. Whither, then, in
the ailing world between the wars, was a man like Christopher Benn to look, however sanguine by nature, unless to
the past?

The backward look had to go beyond the nineteenth
century, the century of the music of the burgessy—a music,
on the one hand, of merely domestic affections and on the
other of adventurous extravagance. The age of the middle
classes was that of spirited adventure. Its sons, sailing

every sea and hacking their way through continents, made
fortunes at the ends of the earth and founded empires by
accident. Berlioz and Wagner represent in music that spirit
of audacious exploration. The *Ring* is a nineteenth-century
empire, magnificent and ramshackle. The middle class
which roamed a half-discovered world was, at the same
time, the class of a special warmheartedness in family rela-
tions. Schumann and Brahms are the musicians of burgess
affections and of the big and close-knit families, where
almost every day is someone's birthday or wedding anni-
versary, fondly observed.

But the wonderful age was over in 1919, and its
splendour was tarnished for the time by the horrors of the
catastrophe in which it fell. Europe's confidence in itself
was undermined, and perhaps more than anywhere else
among the victorious nations of the West. It is illustrative
of the scepticism of the time that there was a moment
when the backward glance of some should have impatiently
passed even over Beethoven, since Beethoven's sombre
heroism was hopeful at heart, and hope was illusion. Some
retreated to the sixteenth century, but in general the order
of the eighteenth, as idealized in Bach and Mozart, was
the chosen refuge.

Bach, perhaps yes—but at the beginning of this century
could anyone have conceived that Mozart would come to
figure on the scene in anything like this imposing way?
It is curious to remember how, in the days before Beecham's
propaganda, little of Mozart's music was currently performed in England. Hardly more than three or four sym-
phonies, or more than four or five concertos; a dozen or so
of the chamber works. At Edwardian Covent Garden only
Don Giovanni was sung. Beecham brought *Così fan Tutte*
back to light; at Drury Lane he enthralled London after

many years with *The Magic Flute*; he made the *Seraglio* into a favourite, a popular opera; he produced *Figaro* in a stylish form which set a new standard for the staging of classical opera in England. All this was at the time an enrichment rather than the meeting of a need. But the day of the absolute need for Mozart was close at hand.

The times turned tragic, and in a world that had lost its bearings Mozart represented man in control of his world. The more the crystal was peered into, the greater seemed the wonder. Divine, the creativeness in that incessant play of sound. But admirable above all, in the light of these latter days, the faultless adequacy; not the springing invention only, but its contained sufficiency and divine completeness—illimitable with never an extravagance! While Mozart's fame had never, in a century and a half, suffered anything like the eclipse that at one time befell Bach, this was a new appreciation.

In the sanguine nineteenth century Mozart was seen as out-topped and overshadowed by Beethoven. Any other view was paradoxical, and Oulibishev an eccentric. Jahn felt bound to magnify all he could find in Mozart of prophetic romanticism. It was his defence of Mozart against the century's image of him, bewigged and dressed in lace and silk. Parry could not altogether overcome this or banish a rococo Mozart, frivolous compared with Beethoven, the fact being that his age had no absolute need of a music earlier than Beethoven's.

The new hour struck, and it brought a task. That was part of the interest and the charm—that the generation had not merely to bask in a restored radiance, but had its own share and endeavour to give to the restoration, the exercise to make of all possible wit and judgment in the practice of Mozart's music. The whirlpool was on the one hand and on the other the sandbanks—to starboard an anachronistic passion and fury of sound, and to port the exaggeration, in deference to the fashion of men's clothes in Mozart's day, of daintiness. *Don Giovanni* had been turned from a merry into a tragic opera, and memories still fresh were of Paderewski's audacious clatter in the march of the Sonata in A major and of Busoni storming in the C minor Fantasia. But it was now the day of the regimen of the historic conscience in musical execution, and perhaps there had never, in the instrumental field at all events, been Mozartian performances at once so richly full and so faithful as in the decades of this retrospect.

Nor, at the same time, had there been scenic productions of the operas so cared for and ingenious. This, a peculiar preoccupation of the age, was the subject of the study upon which Christopher Benn was engaged in the years before 1939 and which is represented substantially by the present book.

What were the effect and character of the original productions of Mozart's operas? We can do rather more than guess. There is the abundance of the eighteenth-century's testimony to the virtuosity of its singers, and we have the first Basilio's, Michael Kelly's, account of *Figaro* in 1786:

> It was allowed that never was opera stronger cast. I have seen it performed at different periods in other countries, and well too, but no more to compare with its original performance than light is to darkness.

A given music is evidence of what was the contemporary executive art, and Mozart exacts a higher proficiency from his singers than from any instrumentalist. From the accounts that have come down of the relentless encoring with which his public, like Sullivan's later on, interrupted

the comedy, we see that, Gluck and his reforms notwith-
standing, what was relished above all was the singing of
the songs; and it may well be that at any superior performance this was of a consistency of style and fineness beyond
anything the Salzburg or Glyndebourne of our days has
been able to present. That we should, after the extrava-
gances of the vocal writing of nineteenth-century composers, have still had good and even, if rarely, some
superlatively good Mozartian singing is wonder enough.

What the ideal of the eighteenth century was in this
respect is clear to see in all the music of the age, but pre-
eminently in Handel and Mozart. It was a style supremely
equable and controlled, and no effect of passion or power
was admissible at the expense of consistent quality of tone.
As did the music itself of the seventeenth and eighteenth
centuries, so did the representative executive art, singing,
exemplify the social ideal of the age, the aristocratic age,
in which superiority expressed itself in untroubled and easy
stateliness of manner, apparently inborn and almost superhuman—or such was the ideal—certainly unattainable by
the trading and toiling multitude. The concurrent abuses
are no longer here or there, but the principal of these is
illustrative. Superhuman in appearance were the manners
of the aristocracy and the effect achieved of freedom from
ordinary mortal cares; and superhuman in effect, if less
than human in its cause, was the representative musical
performance, peculiar to the time, the art which was
admired above all and which was an exemplar for all
ordinarily equipped singers—that, namely, of the idolized
Italian castrati, a class whose extinction has meant that
much of Handel's music, do what the normally equipped
can with such a piece as *Semele,* has become a nearly dead
letter. The grandest music of the baroque age was in-

15

spired by what must have been an incomparable vocal art —incomparable in the combination of power and mellifluousness, and angelic-seeming, so the witnesses testify, in its serenity and unearthly detachment.[1] Singers of both sexes emulated this style, particularly of course in serious music; but the singing of merry music, too, was influenced by the ideal of sustained control, excluding all roughness and inequality. What we usually get now in the performance of a grand aria of the aristocratic period is a reversal of the original effect—an instrumental obbligato supermundane, angelic, and then human frailty in the song. When Mozart composed for his "molto amato castrato Dal Prato," the end of the day of these emasculated singers was nearing, but their art set its seal on all his vocal music, and not there only, but on every adagio he ever wrote.

What the next age brought was an enormous exaggeration of passionate expression in vocal music, at the price of qualitative imperfection. Rossini and Verdi demanded ever more vehemence and forcefulness. The Germans were still more exorbitant. Wagner's way of representing Valhallan divinities was to charge mortal shoulders with loads unbearable. In Straussian opera the singers are Laocoöns desperately entangled and overpowered. With Schoenberg, at the end of the chapter, song becomes feline miaowing. To all these demands there was an heroic response, and it is a saying that never has an indifferent performance been known of *Elektra* or *Pierrot Lunaire*. How admirable, then, that the style of

[1] See, for instance, in *Peregrine Pickle*, Lydia Melford's account of a concert at Ranelagh: "There I heard the famous Tenducci. . . . The voice, to be sure, is neither man's nor woman's; but it is more melodious than either; and it warbled so divinely that, while I listened, I really thought myself in paradise."

the century of Handel and Mozart should still not have been lost sight of! Though the new age demanded of its singers feats analogous to the exploration of Darkest Africa —so must the exactions of *Tristan* have at first appeared —they were not all or wholly engrossed in romantic adventure.

The genius of Bach, Handel and Mozart maintained awareness in the world of another music, ideally lofty and serene, and the tradition of its vocal style survived. Forty years ago Melba's singing of "L'amerò, sarò costante" and the Zerlina songs, and Battistini's of "Non più andrai" were purely, perfectly Mozartian. Nothing of quite that pre-eminence, it is true, distinguished the new Mozartian movement between the wars; yet, if the singing was not the glory of the movement, it must be said to have been generally pleasing and sometimes beautifully fine—certainly never affected by the peculiar vocal developments required by the contemporary school of composition.

But the fact was that singing was no longer the focus of interest. It could not be, by reason, for one thing, of the very fervour of the movement. To focus endeavour on fine Mozartian singing would have been to tread too obsequiously in footprints made by the insuperable past. In the art of music there is a secondary creativeness, that of the interpreter or executant, who shares the glory of a great creative period. What he, as well as the composer, has striven for and achieved is something new, a discovery and conquest. Thus along with Handel his interpreters attained breadths of majesty never known before; Mozart's, a realm of new radiancy; Beethoven's (though here the secondary art no doubt lagged somewhat), an arena of heroic energies without example in music.

If in the new age, which was but partially and inadequately interested by its own composers, Mozart was to be called upon to meet the need, what could interpretation do that would be not unenterprizing imitation or reproduction but somehow creative? One answer was found in a reconsideration of the operas and their presentation as scenic entities. There was *Figaro*—not merely a vessel brimming with the sweetest and most sparkling music in the world, but a comedy of consummate construction, rich in characters and faultless in its intricate design. There was *Così fan Tutte*, hardly less admirable in its different way: a slight but perfectly elegant design, marvellously illuminated and vivified by a musical invention which, all the time, observed the slightness of the proposition. More enticing still, with all their imperfection of framework, were the even more wonderful *Don Giovanni* and *The Magic Flute*; for the very shortcomings of structure were a challenge, an occasion for ingenious persuasion and disguise, if Mozartian opera was to be presented no longer as a sort of costumed concert but a dramatic whole.

Like Beecham's productions, Edward Dent's book on Mozart's operas, published in 1913, came prophetically. It threw out any number of suggestions—upon the seriousness, for instance, of the content of *The Magic Flute*, which it had been the accepted thing to think of as hardly more than nonsensical pantomime, accidentally glorified by divine songs. Then there had been the Mozart productions at the Munich summer festivals, in many ways scrupulous and engaging, although rendered rather provincial-seeming from the general European point of view by the practice of translating the Italian operas into German, a language which introduces into the sound an alien element, one remarkably less compatible with the music, in point of fact, than English.

INTRODUCTION

One *Don Giovanni* of those Munich days comes back to mind, altogether more subdued in colouring than the production usually is, and for the most part suffused with moonlight. It is, indeed, an opera of night scenes, apart from one series in the first act, though the producer inclines as a rule to counter the effect of this by the brilliant illumination of interiors. At Munich that year, so I seem to remember, brilliance was avoided, and the result was something dream-like. The characters were all rather ghostly; all, that is to say, save an exceptionally robust and earthy Leporello; and the effect was that the whole action became a dream, Leporello's dream. A typical modern ingenuity! Christopher Benn takes up the suggestion in his chapter on *Don Giovanni*, when he says that not Don Giovanni but Leporello is the central figure of the opera, which "may be regarded as Leporello's dream"; though he does not wholly adopt the view, or he would hardly tackle so seriously the difficulty of the chronology in the last few scenes of the second act. For what has chronology to do with a dream?

The sort of question that was debated in the days we are looking back upon arose over the conventional introduction of a couple of courtesans into the scene of Don Giovanni's last supper. This detail seems to have been of long standing in Germany, and it was accepted at Glyndebourne, where German influences were prevalent. Benn was too faithful an adherent of Glyndebourne to condemn it out of hand, but he mentions the objections, most forcibly put by Rouché. Don Giovanni is not a sultan out to recruit a harem; he is a hunter, not a collector.

A question which the reader of the general discussion may put is why, if fidelity to the composer's genius was the first of considerations, the governing principle has not been approximation to the scenic picture of his time; and it is a question to which point has been given by some of the century's productions of *Don Giovanni*, for instance, loaded with exaggerated Spanish baroque decoration, and *The Magic Flute* transported into the aridity of a world of cubes. But if one thing more than another is irrecoverable from the past, it is its theatrical practice. Fancy may play with the soft harmonies of colour produced by candle-light gleaming on eighteenth-century silk and embroidery, and may see the electric brilliance of *Figaro,* in modern representation, as gaudy. But this is the electrical age, and the law would prohibit a candle-lighted Covent Garden. Not only the fierce lighting of our scenes makes demands on production unknown in the other age, but also the frame of mind of a public habitually dazzled by the new diversion of the time, the moving-picture screen. Only a generation ago, and the word "photogenic" had not been coined. It stands for something the opera house cannot leave out of account. Not only does anything much less than the glare of the screen spell dullness; but also the eye, habituated to impersonations always and eminently photogenic, is promoted to be first critic at the operatic spectacle. With what result? Our boasted Mozartian productions are less than true to their intentions. The real, the glowing radiance lies in the music, but a cold ferocity of mechanical light has to be allowed to vie with it. The ear is relegated to second place. The Juliet of Melba's maturity would to-day be judged by the appearance of her person and considered to want verisimilitude; between the claims of mature vocal art and girlish beauty there must be a compromise, and the finer singer of "Dove sono" is apt to lose the part of Rosina to the more photogenic. The beautiful Mozartian

productions of the time have, in brief, been rather too
highly coloured and not quite superlatively sung.

Almost inevitably, as we have seen. But Christopher
Benn had a practical mind that did not go looking for
midi à quatorze heures. He appreciated enthusiastically
the brilliant achievements of Glyndebourne and the wit
that went to the making of each opera a whole "convincing to the modern audience." The reader of his book will
learn of many of the problems and their solution, and will
find an enhanced interest in his next attendance at a
Mozart opera.

*   *   *   *   *

After Bagûsh I saw my friend no more. The battle
broke; the scene for everyone moved westward, to
Cyrenaica. One December day there came to me, lying
in a hole in the sand, sick with a desert pleurisy, news of
disaster. Alf Bowman, out on a mission to our garrison
at the Cyrenaican oasis of Jalo, had been shot down—the
Tasmanian Bowman, a lionheart of the Desert Air Force,
a man whom to know was to know the spirit of valour
incarnate, to know Hector. And with him in the aircraft
was Christopher Benn.

RICHARD CAPELL.

ATHENS,
December 1945.

I

LE NOZZE DI FIGARO

LE NOZZE DI FIGARO
(The Marriage of Figaro)

Opera buffa in Four Acts, by Lorenzo Da Ponte

Count Almaviva	Baritone
The Countess	Soprano
Susanna	Soprano
Figaro	Bass
Cherubino	Soprano
Marcellina	Contralto
Basilio	Tenor
Don Curzio	Tenor
Bartolo	Bass
Antonio	
Barbarina	Soprano

The scene is laid in Seville.

The opera was first produced in Vienna on May 1st, 1786.

SYNOPSIS OF THE STORY

ACT I

The Room of Figaro and Susanna

Figaro measures the room for furniture, while Susanna tries on a new hat. It is their wedding-day. He is delighted with the room, but Susanna is suspicious of the Count's "generosity" in giving them a room so near to his own, and warns Figaro of the Count's intentions towards her. She goes out to answer the Countess's bell; Figaro, fired by jealousy, determines not to let the Count have the upper hand. He goes off, and Bartolo and Marcellina enter. Marcellina has a bond from Figaro, given to secure a loan, whereby he has promised to repay the money to her or in default to marry her. Bartolo agrees to assist her in approaching the Count to get

25

her bond fulfilled. Bartolo leaves the stage, and Susanna returns. She and Marcellina exchange abusive compliments as Marcellina goes off.

As soon as Susanna is left alone, Cherubino comes in to tell Susanna that the Count has sent him away because he found him alone with Barbarina. He begs her to persuade the Countess, with whom he imagines himself to be in love, to intercede for him. He steals from Susanna a ribbon belonging to the Countess, and in exchange gives her a Canzonetta which he has composed. They are disturbed by the arrival of the Count, and Cherubino therefore hides behind the big armchair. The Count makes love to Susanna and suggests a meeting in the garden. Before the Count receives an answer, Basilio comes in. The Count gets behind the chair, while Cherubino climbs round the front and hides in it, Susanna covering him with the Count's cloak. Basilio regales her with all the gossip of the household, but when he talks of Cherubino's unashamed flirtations with the Countess, the Count can contain himself no longer, and jumps out from his hiding-place. Susanna is terrified and pretends to faint. When the men suggest putting her into the chair, she quickly comes round. Basilio, who has seen the Page hidden in the chair, sarcastically assures the Count that his remarks about Cherubino were merely an invention, but the Count is adamant, and in spite of Basilio's and Susanna's entreaties for him, declares that Cherubino must go.

The Count explains that he found Cherubino hidden under the table-cloth in the cottage when he went to see Barbarina, the gardener's daughter. By way of demonstration he lifts the cloak from the chair, only to find Cherubino hidden again. Basilio is delighted, but the Count realizes that Cherubino has overheard his amorous conversation with Susanna. The Count calls for Figaro to be fetched, to witness for himself his bride's treachery. To the Count's amazement Susanna is not in the least afraid for Figaro to know what has happened, for her conscience is absolutely clear. Figaro at this moment arrives with a party of peasants from the estate, who acclaim the Count's magnanimity in renouncing his feudal *jus primae noctis*. Figaro suggests that his marriage should take place at once, but the Count, for no good reason, postpones the ceremony. He further says that he will give Cherubino a commission in his regiment. Figaro and Susanna are now left alone

26

with Cherubino, and Figaro paints for the Page a lurid picture of his new life as a soldier.

Act II

The Apartments of the Countess

The Countess, alone, prays to the god of love to restore her lost happiness. Susanna joins her and tells of the Count's advances towards her. Figaro comes in and outlines his plan to defeat the Count. He will give Basilio a letter purporting to come from Susanna, to give to the Count, suggesting a meeting in the garden. The appointment will be kept by Cherubino, attired in Susanna's clothes. The plan is approved, and Figaro goes off, sending the Page in to be dressed for the escapade. Cherubino now sings his Canzonetta, and Susanna sets about dressing him up. When she has finished she goes off, but the Countess and Cherubino are soon disturbed by the Count, unexpectedly returned from the hunt. Cherubino is hustled into the inner room, and the trembling Countess unlocks the door to admit her husband. He at once suspects his wife, and is told that Susanna is in the inner room. At this moment Susanna slips in unnoticed and hides behind the screen in front of the Countess's bed. The Count shouts through the inner door, which is locked, telling Susanna to come out. Eventually he takes the Countess out, locking the main door as they go, to fetch tools to break open the inner door. In their absence Susanna calls Cherubino out of the inner room, and as the only means of escape, he jumps out of the window. Susanna then takes his place in the inner room.

On their return, the Countess admits to her husband that Cherubino is in the inner room and gives him the key. Both are therefore confused when Susanna comes out of the inner door just as the Count is about to open it. The Count appears to be beaten, but he remembers the letter, which Basilio has given to him. Susanna and the Countess admit that this was concocted by Figaro to be given to him by Basilio, and disarmed by this admission, the Count makes peace with his wife. At this moment Figaro bursts in, eager for his wedding to take place at once. The Count questions him about the letter. He at first denies all knowledge of it but when the others tell him that the Count already knows its origin, he admits his part in the plot.

There now seems to be no excuse for the further postponement of the wedding, but the Count is saved by the entrance of Antonio, the gardener, who complains that someone has jumped out of the window and smashed his carnations. Figaro knows that it was the Page, for he saw him, but in a desperate effort to get out of a difficult position, he says that it was he who jumped out. Antonio at once produces the Page's officer's patent, which was dropped as he jumped. This time the fat is properly in the fire, until the Countess notices that the patent has not been sealed, and Figaro is able to extricate himself by saying that the Page gave it to him to have it sealed. The sudden entry of Marcellina, Bartolo, and Basilio, who come to present Marcellina's claims upon Figaro to the Count, enables the Count to postpone the wedding once more.

ACT III

Scene 1. *A Room in the Castle*

The Count ruminates upon the curious events of the day, when Susanna comes in, sent by the Countess to make a rendezvous in the garden with him, which she herself intends to keep, dressed in Susanna's clothes. She makes the rendezvous, and as she goes out, she tells Figaro that their cause is won. This remark is overheard by the Count, who consoles himself with thoughts of revenge upon Figaro. Don Curzio, the lawyer, then comes in to announce his decision that Figaro must marry Marcellina in default of repayment of the debt. Figaro argues that he cannot marry without his parents' consent, and then Bartolo and Marcellina recognize him as their long-lost son, who was stolen from them at birth. General rejoicing follows this discovery, only the Count having cause for anger. When they have all gone, Barbarina arranges with Cherubino to dress him up as a girl, so that he may further delay his departure for Seville, whither he has been ordered by the Count. After this the Countess comes in, thinking once again of her unhappiness. After she has left the stage, Antonio tells the Count that Cherubino is still in the castle.

and produces his officer's hat, found in his cottage, as proof. Then the Countess dictates a letter to Susanna to be given to the Count to confirm the rendezvous. The letter is sealed with a pin which is to be returned to the sender. This done, Barbarina brings in a party of girls with flowers for the Countess, among them Cherubino dressed up. The girls' song is interrupted by Antonio and the Count, who recognize Cherubino. Barbarina pleads for him and asks that she may marry him, to which the Count agrees. Figaro then appears, and when the wedding march strikes up they all prepare for the ceremony.

Scene 2. *The Wedding Room*

Bartolo and Marcellina are to be married as well as Figaro and Susanna, and both bridal pairs pass before the Count and Countess. As she goes by Susanna slips the letter into the Count's hand. He pricks himself with the pin with which it is sealed, and this is observed by Figaro.

Act IV

The Garden

Figaro and Marcellina find Barbarina looking for the pin, which she tells them was given to her by the Count to return to Susanna. Figaro remembers the letter which the Count had in his hand during the wedding ceremony, and suspects that it must have come from Susanna. Barbarina ingenuously confirms this, and tells Figaro that the Count has arranged to meet Susanna by the pine-trees. Figaro is furious, and goes off to seek revenge, in spite of Marcellina's counsel of moderation. She believes that Susanna is innocent, and decides to warn her of Figaro's suspicions. Barbarina comes in again, this time bringing fruit for Cherubino, whom she is to meet in one of the rotundas. She is observed by Figaro, who comes with Bartolo and Basilio, whom he has brought to witness his wife's meeting with the Count. He arranges that they shall hide, and shall emerge from their hiding-places when he gives the signal. Figaro goes off to complete his plans. In his absence Basilio sings a song and then takes up his position with Bartolo.

All Figaro's plans are now laid to catch Susanna in the midst of her treachery. He returns to the stage and expresses his bitter disappointment at Susanna's conduct, and warns other men to beware of women. He hides, and Susanna and the Countess come and exchange their cloaks, assisted by Marcellina, who warns them that Figaro is in hiding and watching them. Figaro does not actually see them changing their cloaks. Marcellina hides, and the Countess goes off to prepare for the arrival of the Count to keep the rendezvous. Susanna now throws off her cloak, so that Figaro may see that it is she, and sings a song expressing her longing for the moment when she is in his arms. Figaro is furious, for he imagines, as she intended him to do, that she is referring to her meeting with the Count. Susanna herself now hides, and the Countess reappears, still dressed as Susanna. She is disturbed by Cherubino, and the Count, on his arrival, is angry to find that the Page has crossed his path again.

Figaro, who has not seen Susanna hide, and who imagines that the disguised Countess is his wife, comes out of his hiding-place at this moment, only to be rewarded with the cuff which the Count intended for Cherubino. The Count now leads the Countess, disguised as Susanna, off to the Rotunda at the top. Figaro emerges again, and Susanna, disguising her voice to sound like the Countess', tells Figaro that she will revenge herself upon her "husband," and suggests that he makes love to her. For an instant she forgets to disguise her voice, and Figaro realizes that it is Susanna. He still plays up to her, however, and makes love to her as if she were the Countess. This game does not last long, and they at once make up their differences, Figaro regretting his mistrust of his wife. When the Count returns, however, Susanna resumes her disguise, and Figaro is caught in the act of making violent love to the supposed Countess. This is the signal for general confusion, and the Count openly accuses Figaro of treachery. The truth comes to light when the Countess herself appears. The Count asks her forgiveness, and all ends happily.

THE OPERA

Le Nozze di Figaro is at once the most popular and the most satisfactory of Mozart's operas. It is based upon Beaumarchais' play *Le Mariage de Figaro*, which was first allowed to be performed in France in 1784, and was still banned in Vienna when Mozart and Da Ponte approached the subject. Da Ponte[1] gives an amusing account of an interview with the Emperor Joseph II, whose permission was required before the opera could be produced. "But," said the Emperor, "I have forbidden the German Company to perform the *Marriage of Figaro*." "Yes," was the reply, "but as I have written a drama for music and not a comedy, I have had to omit many scenes, and shorten many more, and I have omitted and shortened those elements which might offend the delicacy and decency of a spectacle at which Your Majesty presides."

No doubt, reflecting on the interview after many years, Da Ponte enlarged upon it when he came to record it in his *Memoirs*. It was an empty assurance, which he gave to the Emperor in order to secure his consent to the performance of the opera. In substance, Da Ponte justly differentiated the opera from the play. The play was written primarily as a political drama, uncompromising in its boldness, and it has come to be known as a forerunner of the French Revolution. Mozart and Da Ponte have removed the play from its original political surroundings, but they have done nothing to rob it of its force. They have emphasized the human and social aspects of the story, and by so doing

[1] Books mentioned in these pages are referred to by the names of the authors, the titles being given in the Bibliography on page 178.

have rendered it timeless. The political significance of Beaumarchais' play is now a matter of past history, but Mozart's opera is immortal, because it portrays the human feelings which are common to all times and to all places. In spite of this, a clear idea of the eighteenth-century outlook is essential to a proper appreciation of the opera. The characters are drawn by showing their reactions one to another, and it is necessary to understand the social life of a nobleman's Court at that time.

The story deals with the Court of Count Almaviva, an aristocrat of the highest rank. His Court is a world in itself, where every branch of life is represented. He would have his administrators on the one hand, and those who catered for his entertainment on the other. All those belonging to the latter class, whether musicians, poets, or mere kitchen boys or stable hands, were servants. Thus in *Le Nozze di Figaro*, the Count and Countess alone represent the highest aristocracy. Against them are set Figaro and Susanna, the personal servants, Basilio the music teacher and Antonio the gardener. These are all menial servants, with no particular distinction of grade. The others are outside the immediate circle of the household. Bartolo is a lawyer, presumably of some respectability, for the Countess was his ward. Marcellina is a little lower in the social grade. She was probably Bartolo's housekeeper and hence his mistress. Cherubino is the Count's Page, but he cannot be of high social standing, for he marries Barbarina, the gardener's daughter. The main protagonists in the opera are the Count, on the one hand, and Figaro and Susanna on the other. The battle between them is a human battle, as opposed to a political battle, which was the essence of the play. Thus although the particular political character of Beaumarchais' play may have disappeared, there still remains, as the vital key to the

Aulikki Rautawaara as THE COUNTESS in *Le Nozze di Figaro*
(Glyndebourne)

opera, the unbridgeable gulf between master and man. The sentiments expressed by Figaro in the opera are not, as in the play, revolutionary from the point of view of a particular political struggle, but are none the less revolutionary. Here for the first time a servant is made the hero, and above all he is made to appear as a real character, with strong feelings which he does not hesitate to express.

The contrast between the Count and Countess and their servants must be apparent at every turn, and can be forcibly underlined by proper attention to costumes and scenery. Too often this contrast is lost in the vague and nondescript atmosphere of the theatrical "eighteenth century." The reality of the world in which the opera is enacted is so vitally portrayed in the music that Figaro's grievances can still be understood. On the other hand, it is much more difficult to-day to understand the motives which govern the conduct of the Count. The key to his behaviour is his *jus primae noctis,* a terrible feudal right which casts a dark shadow over the lives of the lower orders. This right is the axis around which the story of the opera revolves. The servants, especially the female servants, are mere chattels of the master, and handled as such by him. In the opera they are human beings, and in consequence the sympathies of the audience are with them.

The story of Figaro begins with Beaumarchais' earlier play, *Le Barbier de Séville.* In this, the young Count Almaviva enlists the support of Figaro, the barber, to abduct Rosina from the house of Bartolo, her guardian. The second play, *Le Mariage de Figaro,* upon which the opera is based, follows directly on the first. Thus in the opera the Count and Countess are a young and fairly recently married couple

THE CHARACTERS

The Count is an unsympathetic figure. He is not intentionally cruel, but is merely a product of the typical upbringing of a nobleman in the decadent age in which he lived. In England the enjoyment of position and property has always been based upon the rendering of services. The tenure of land and the rights which it involved were, and are, dependent upon duty. This sense of duty has never been wholly lost sight of, with the result that a violent revolution such as occurred in France in 1789 has been avoided. The French aristocracy of the eighteenth century, of whom Almaviva, although nominally translated to Spain, is a typical example, were in a different position. Their regime was one of tyranny, and in consequence their overthrow was ruthless. Almaviva is the victim of his age. Complacent and unimaginative in the extreme, he does not perhaps realize that he is cruel. He thinks of nothing but himself and the subjection of his household to his will. This is a bitter, but no means exaggerated, portrait of the Grand Seigneur.

The Countess is a weak figure, and her very weakness excites pity. She cannot be blamed, as a young and inexperienced girl, for having been swept off her feet by Almaviva's ardent suit. A few years of married life have served to make him tired of her, but it is no fault of hers, if, through inexperience, she has failed to retain his affection. She is still young, for Cherubino would scarcely pay so much attention to her if she were middle-aged, nor for that matter could she convincingly change clothes with Susanna in the last Act. She is more human than her husband, and more sympathetic, perhaps because—a bitter reflection—she is not so well bred. She is entirely dependent upon the support and guidance of Susanna, who directs her every action, and at last wins back for her the love of her husband.

Susanna is the central figure of the opera. Without her sane guidance and moderating influence Figaro would not succeed in overcoming the Count. Her love for Figaro is the basis of her character. This is the firm rock upon which she builds, and she can consequently afford to regard the Count's intentions upon her with dispassionate aloofness. She guides Figaro at every turn, allaying his unfounded suspicions and piloting his ideas into the right channels. She guides the Countess, and above all she knows how to handle the Count, leading him on just far enough to enable her to make him do exactly what she wants. She is in no sense of the word a coquette, far from it. Observe that she never "flirts" with anyone. In the first Act the attentions of Basilio and the Count are terrifying to her. For Cherubino she has the sympathetic regard of an older sister, to whom he turns for advice. Only in the third Act, and then strictly in pursuance of the agreed plan of action, does she approach the Count, and deceive him into thinking that she is as clay in his hands, to mould as he chooses. Her love for Figaro is a factor ignored by the Count in his schemings, but it is a love which proves too powerful for him. Throughout the opera her time is fully taken up in dealing with each situation as it arises. Only at the end, in her Rose aria, is she seen in repose. This aria reveals the genuineness and depth of her character, and must of itself be sufficient to belie a coquettish interpretation of the part.

Figaro himself was the local barber in *Le Barbier de Séville*. Now he is in Almaviva's employ as personal servant. As the barber, his trade gave him the entrée to all the noble houses, including that of Bartolo, and consequently he was a valuable ally of Almaviva in his abduction of Rosina. In the previous play Figaro directed the operations and made the plans. His methods were direct and very crude, but were none the less successful in defeating Bartolo. Here the problem is not so simple. The arrangement of an elopement from the house of a fool was easy, but the defeat of the Count in the delicate matter of his feudal rights is another picture. Figaro approaches the new problem with the same technique as before, and does not appreciate that more subtlety and finesse will be required to defeat the Count. His enthusiasm is the driving force still, but now it is directed by Susanna. Figaro is essentially an honest and straightforward character; a man who gives, and expects to receive, the best from everyone. At once in the opening scene this facet of his character is revealed. He enthusiastically accepts the room which the Count has allotted to him, and Susanna has the utmost difficulty in making him see the Count's sinister motives. In his Cavatina, Figaro's indignation is boiling over. His fury for the moment is wild, and has not yet been harnessed by Susanna. Figaro is the best of men; his motives are honest, and his intentions good, but he is slow in the uptake and not unnaturally jealous.

In Beaumarchais' play Bartolo was a physician, but in the opera he has become a lawyer. The transformation serves to add point to his support of Marcellina's claims upon Figaro. At the beginning of the opera he still clings to a certain respectability, but he slowly declines, and eventually his past history is revealed in all its disreputable detail. He has to acknowledge Figaro, the servant, as his son, and recognizes Marcellina's right to be his wife. Marcellina must be an old and unattractive woman, for she is Figaro's mother and Bartolo's long-since-discarded mistress.

Cherubino's youth is no longer the excuse that it once was for spending his time pursuing every female in the palace. He realizes this, but makes himself out to be younger and more innocent than he really is, for he is reluctant to relinquish his position as the spoilt baby of the family. The Count deems it necessary to take drastic action to secure his absence, thereby admitting him as a serious rival.

THE PRODUCTION

Le Nozze di Figaro is in no sense a farce. It has perhaps come to be so regarded because it is described as an opera buffa. This is not the place for a discussion of the history of opera buffa; for this the reader is referred to Jahn.[1] Suffice it to say that opera buffa is a technical term describing the manner and style in which the opera is written, and is not to be translated "comic opera" in the Gilbert and Sullivan sense. The inevitable association of Mozart's opera with Rossini's Barbiere di Siviglia may also to some extent account for the treatment of the former as a farce. Rossini's opera is also an opera buffa, being constructed musically on the same technical basis, but it is a comic opera in the above sense, which Mozart's is not. Le Nozze di Figaro, then, is an intense drama, and its reality is brought out in every page of the music. A stylized "powdered wig" production detracts from the full force of the opera, but while the music should be played as dramatically as possible, attention must nevertheless be paid to the style of the production. Over-insistence upon

[1] See also Professor Dent's footnotes to pages 66 and 67.

elegance has, in the past, led to a fatal weakening of the force of the drama, but a certain elegant formality of manner may yet be combined with dramatic intensity.

ACT I

The opera opens with the room in the palace which the Count has allotted to his servant Figaro, in which he is to live with Susanna. It is the servants' quarters, and the eighteenth century, in the days before popular education and enlightenment. It is a mistake, as is often done, to stage this scene in a beautiful room, entirely uncontrasted with the later scenes in the apartments of the Count and Countess. In this case there is nothing extraordinary in the conduct of the various characters who pass in and out. The Count appears to be quite at home in such a beautiful room, indistinguishable from his own: the whole point of the scene is thus lost, and the significance of what follows after is lost with it. Why should Figaro be measuring the room for furniture if it be already tastefully and completely furnished? If the intrigue is to have any point, it should be patently obvious from the first moment of entry that the Count is compromising himself by the mere fact of being seen in the room at all. Dent[1] refers to a production in which this room was "nothing more than the shapeless space concealed behind the semi-circular partition forming the apse of some unseen throne-room."

At Glyndebourne the scene is made out of a passage. The Count's and Countess's apartments are on either side, and at the back is a French window apparently leading to the garden. The passage combines both the elements

[1] Page 183.

necessary for this scene. In the first place it is abun,
clear that the "room" has just been made up of an
space, and is extremely inconvenient for its occupants, an
yet conveniently near for their master and mistress. In
the second place, as a passage rather than a definite room,
there is nothing extraordinary in the continuous flow of
people in and out of the room. It is apparent that there
is no privacy to be enjoyed by its occupants, and the
accessibility of Susanna to each and every male philanderer
justifies Figaro's jealousy later on. The only furniture
required for the scene is a big armchair and a dressing-
table, or mirror of some sort, for Susanna. There should
be no more than this, for Figaro and Susanna have not yet
moved in, and Figaro is measuring the room for the other
furniture, which will no doubt be supplied later from the
odds and ends of the palace "box-room." The dirty faded
wallpaper, with patches unfaded indicating where pictures
once hung, adds to the uncomfortable atmosphere.

When the curtain rises Figaro is wholly absorbed with
his measuring and Susanna is trying on her hat in front
of the mirror. She vainly tries to interest Figaro, but he
goes on with his measuring, assuring her without even
bothering to look that her hat suits her perfectly. It is
a mistake for Figaro to look up from his work until
a little later, when he says, *Or è più bello* ("Yes,
it is lovely"). Their second duet, as has already been
mentioned, clearly underlines the characters of Figaro and
Susanna. Figaro is prepared to accept the gift of the room
as a spontaneous act of generosity on the part of the
Count. He does not impute any sinister motive to his
master. Susanna is more alive to the realities of the situation, and tells Figaro just enough to make him realize the
gravity of the intrigue that he will have to combat. Note

the music of this duet. Both Figaro and Susanna sing the same musical phrase. Figaro sings it in a straightforward and unconcerned way. Mozart turns it round and gives it just a twist to express Susanna's suspicions and fears of the Count's motives.

The appearance of Bartolo and Marcellina is an essential part of the unfolding of the complicated plot. Bartolo's aria in praise of vengeance is a perfect portrait of the pompous lawyer. He should sing it in all seriousness, for Mozart is laughing at him, not with him. On the face of it his anxiety to secure justice for Marcellina is most praiseworthy, but his real motive is to revenge himself upon Figaro. He has not forgotten that Figaro was largely instrumental in procuring the elopement of Rosina, his ward, whom he had hoped to marry himself. His revenge will be complete if he can make Figaro marry Marcellina, and he himself will then be free from the claims that she has upon him. In her little duet with Susanna, the baser side of Marcellina's character is revealed. It is only fair to her to remember that, when she later discovers that she is Figaro's mother, she takes her daughter-in-law completely into her confidence, and at once buries their past jealousy. With the entry of Cherubino, Susanna's troubles begin. Now it is clear why she objects to this room, in which she can expect no privacy, and where she is easy prey for the Count. When he comes in, the Count carries a cloak, and the chair and this cloak provide the necessary facilities for hiding him and Cherubino in turn.

The events that follow serve at once to show Susanna's real character, and to indicate the sort of base treatment to which a girl in her position must be expected to be sub-jected. On a true view of these incidents, there is no room for interpreting the part of Susanna as a coquette. Cherubino is unimportant, but Susanna is genuinely terrified of the Count, and is pathetically powerless to get rid of him. She is deeply in love with Figaro, and yet is expected to subject herself, without protest, to the amorous advances of the Count. She is not frightened of Basilio, but this garrulous intriguer will not leave her alone. All and sundry consider themselves at liberty to stroll in and out of her room as they please, and she is impotent to prevent them. When the Count has emerged, and has discovered Cherubino, Susanna can only proclaim her innocence in vain, because for the moment everything seems to be against her. She knows, however, that her conscience is clear, and that she is the helpless victim of cruelty and intrigue. When the Count calls for Figaro, she knows that he will trust her, and that she has no cause for anxiety. Figaro's appearance, with a party of young people from the estate, diverts the Count's attention from Susanna. This is Figaro's first attempt to defeat the Count. His idea is that his wedding shall be the first to take place under the new régime, that is, since the Count abandoned his feudal *jus primae noctis*. He brings in the party of people as witnesses in the hope of getting from the Count a public renunciation of his rights. He is successful in this, and the Count can only weakly postpone the wedding until later. The chorus is sung the first time with gusto and enthusiasm, the second time with bitter sarcasm to mark the general resentment at the postponement of the wedding.

The Act concludes with Figaro's mock military aria, during which Susanna must be kept on the stage effectively employed. At Glyndebourne she busies herself searching through a trunk for Figaro's old military cloak and hat, in which she dresses Cherubino. This is most appropriate, for a trunk of clothes not yet put away would be expected to be part of the paraphernalia of moving in. Towards the end of the aria she and Figaro take Cherubino's arm, and march him up and down the stage, until he breaks away from them in a fury. Let it not be forgotten that Cherubino loathes every minute of Figaro's bitter teasing. There is no question of him marching up and down with enthusiasm during the aria. His appointment to an Officer's commission means banishment from the castle, and he is not at all pleased with his new rank. "Don't call me by that terrible name," he says soon afterwards.

Act II

In the first Act the importance of creating the right atmosphere in the scenery was considered. Here the problem is not to find the right atmosphere for the scene, which must be ravishingly beautiful, but to arrange the window and doors of the room satisfactorily. According to the text of the opera, there is a window, a screen in front of the Countess's bed, and three doors. The first door is the main entrance to the room, the second leads to an inner room, probably a boudoir, and the third leads to the room of Figaro and Susanna, which was the scene of Act I. These doors are of great importance in the working out of the plot. The text of the opera envisages their use in the following manner.

When the curtain rises the Countess is alone. Susanna joins her, entering by the door from her own room. Figaro enters by the main door, likewise Cherubino. When Susanna has dressed him, she goes in to her own room. The Count knocks at the main door and the Countess locks Cherubino into the inner room, keeping the key herself. She then lets the Count in by the main door, and presently Susanna slips in from her own room, and hides behind the screen. The Count and Countess go out of the main door, and in their absence Cherubino comes from the inner room, and escapes out of the window. Susanna then locks herself into the inner room. The Count and Countess return, and the Countess gives her husband the key to unlock the inner room door, from which Susanna emerges. For the remainder of the scene only the main door is used.

There are two difficulties inherent in this scheme. In the first place, there is nothing to prevent Cherubino from escaping into Susanna's room instead of jumping out of the window. Secondly, the Countess locks Cherubino into the inner room, and she keeps the key, for she still has it in her hand to give to the Count. In this case it is impossible for Cherubino to let himself out and for Susanna to lock herself in, unless it be supposed that there is another key which is kept in the inner room.

The first difficulty is overcome at Glyndebourne by the simple and effective plan of leaving out the door into Susanna's room. This plan involves only one difficulty which will be discussed later on. It must therefore be supposed that the Countess's bedroom and the inner boudoir form a suite by themselves, and that Susanna's room is near at hand along the passage out of the main door.[1]

The key difficulty can only be overcome in the following way. It must be supposed that there are two keys. Cherubino then locks the door on the inside when he goes

[1] There is one feature of the Glyndebourne production which is inconsistent with this plan. In Act I, when Susanna returns for her scene with Marcellina, she is made to curtsy off the stage as she comes in at the door, as if she were curtseying to the Countess. This implies that the two rooms adjoin.

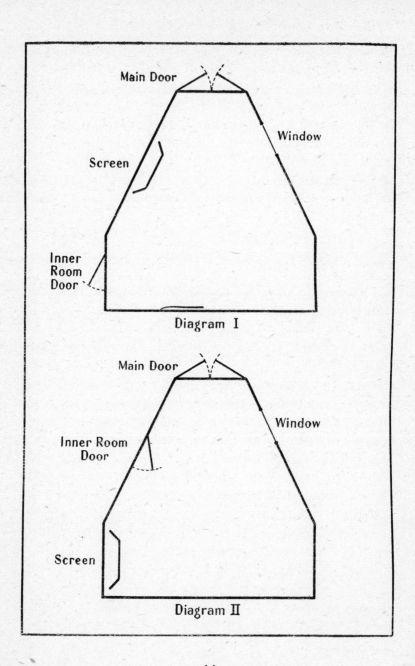

Main Door

Window

Screen

Inner
Room
Door

Diagram I

Main Door

Window

Inner Room
Door

Screen

Diagram II

44

into the inner room, and the locking of the door on the outside by the Countess must be omitted. In this case it is possible for Cherubino to let himself out, and for Susanna to lock herself into the room. Later, when the Count demands the key from the Countess, she must go to a drawer and fetch another key to give to him. Just as the Count comes to open the door Susanna unlocks it from the inside, and opens the door herself. The key is omitted altogether in the Glyndebourne production, but it is submitted that the above method provides a reasonable solution of the problem and does not in any way violate the text.

The two doors and the screen in front of the Countess's bed must be carefully arranged. Their positions in the Glyndebourne scene are illustrated in Diagram I. The main door and the window must clearly be at the back of the stage, but it is suggested that the door into the inner room and the screen would be better placed as shown in Diagram II. As the screen is placed at present, it is necessary for Susanna to peer round it each time she sings, and for the Count and Countess to turn their backs upon it in order to avoid seeing her. These difficulties would be overcome by placing the screen down-stage in the left-hand[1] corner, so that the audience can see behind it, but those on the stage cannot. All Susanna's remarks are asides, and can thus be addressed straight to the audience. In addition, with the screen down-stage, the musical balance of the trio is more easily maintained.

The door into the inner room is the most important feature of the scene. Upon this door is concentrated the Count's fury, and from it, at the most dramatic moment in the Act, Susanna emerges instead of Cherubino. In the

[1] Throughout this book right and left are as seen from the auditorium.

Glyndebourne scene (Diagram I) this door is not clearly visible. It is suggested that it would be better placed as in Diagram II, farther up-stage, and yet not too far to enable the Count to make his assault upon it without turning his back upon the audience.

At the beginning of the Act the Countess is standing by the window, through which the sun pours in upon her. It is surely wrong to make her sit at a dressing-table during her opening Cavatina, as has been done in some productions. Her song is sad and contemplative, and the toilet is scarcely the moment for such deep reflection. In Beaumarchais' play the Countess appears in the first Act, but Mozart and Da Ponte have kept her out of that sordid intrigue. In doing so they have underlined her fundamental character. It is only with reluctance that she takes part in the plan to win back her husband, and she is the only character in the opera who is innocent of any desire to scheme. She has led a secluded life, and is ignorant of the ways of the world. At first she is too taken aback to express an opinion on Figaro's idea of dressing up Cherubino, and sending him to keep the rendezvous with the Count: she can only turn to Susanna for guidance. Her innocence in regard to Cherubino is obvious from the first. She is amused rather than flattered by his ardent attentions, and there is nothing whatever in her conduct to justify the Count's fury.

The staging of Cherubino's Canzonetta at Glynde-bourne is worth mentioning. The song is accompanied by Susanna on the guitar, and in many productions no attempt is made to make Susanna's part in the least realistic, and it is patently obvious that she is not playing at all. At Glyndebourne she sits on a stool with her back to the audience, while the Countess holds the music for her.

For the eye, her accompaniment is thus absolutely convincing. This is a detail of production, in itself unimportant; but the persistent neglect of such details has given to opera generally the reputation for unconvincing staging. When Susanna comes to dress up Cherubino for his meeting with the Count, the Countess retires behind the screen, and Cherubino kneels on a cushion with his back to the audience. He tries all the time to catch a glimpse of the Countess, and Susanna continually has to remind him to pay attention to her. Susanna stands in front of him arranging his clothes, and she thus holds the centre of the stage for her aria. After this, when she has tied up Cherubino's arm, Susanna leaves the stage. She is absent when the Count's premature return disturbs the Countess and Cherubino, and when she comes back and slips behind the screen, she does not know what has happened, and is ignorant of the fact that Cherubino is in the inner room. During the trio she guesses what has occurred.

According to the text of the opera, Susanna should go in and out on this occasion by the door into her own room. At Glyndebourne, of course, this door is left out, and therefore in Professor Ebert's production Susanna remains on the stage all the time. She assists the Countess to hide Cherubino, and slips behind the screen when the Count comes in. This plan makes Susanna's words nonsensical. When she gets behind the screen she says *Il paggio dove andò?* ("Where has the Page gone"?), which is absurd if she has been on the stage all the time. It is submitted that it would be possible for Susanna to leave the stage and to return again by the main door at the back. This is not done at Glyndebourne, because it is supposed that in going out Susanna would meet the Count in the passage, and that in coming in she would make too much noise with the big door, and be observed entering by the Count and Countess. There is no substance in the first of these points, for the Count does not appear until some time after Susanna leaves. The second point is certainly difficult, particularly if Susanna has to go right down the stage to the screen in its altered position (Diagram II, page 44). On the other hand, the Count is so preoccupied with his wife that it should be possible for Susanna to enter and cross the stage to the screen without being observed.

The importance of the visibility of the inner door is seen when the Count and Countess have returned with the tools, and the Countess has given the key to her husband. The Count draws his sword, and just as he is about to open the door, Susanna herself opens it from the inside. The music mounts up to a terrific climax to the moment when the door is opened. It should swing open on to the stage, revealing Susanna framed in the doorway. She need not move until the music changes to Molto Andante, and then she struts forward to curtsey to the Count. If the door is invisible, she must run out at once, and the effect is spoiled.

Little more need be said of the staging of the rest of the Act, but one important point of grouping may be mentioned, as an instructive example of Professor Ebert's technique of producing. At the end of the Act, when Bartolo and Marcellina and Basilio rush in to present Marcellina's claims to the Count, the latter is already on the stage with Figaro and Susanna and the Countess. Here are the two opposing forces, who are at war with each other throughout the early part of the opera. On the one hand are Figaro and Susanna, who are desperately anxious to defeat the Count's intrigue with Susanna and to get

Salvatore Baccaloni as BARTOLO in *Le Nozze di Figaro*
(Glyndebourne)

married. Their principal assistant is the Countess. These three characters are fighting a continual battle with the Count—Figaro, because he can only get married with the Count's permission; Susanna, because she realizes that her marriage to Figaro will alone secure her in some measure from the Count's cruelty; the Countess, because she now realizes that she cannot win her husband back unless she can show him up openly, and make him ashamed of his callous treatment of her.

On the other side are Bartolo, Marcellina and Basilio. Bartolo is still bitterly resentful of Figaro, and is also anxious to be rid of Marcellina by planting her upon Figaro. Marcellina flatters herself that she will succeed in marrying Figaro, and Basilio, the unscrupulous intriguer, is ready to lend his assistance to her cause. The policy of these three is to defeat Figaro in his desire to marry Susanna, and to discredit Susanna's integrity. They also are entirely dependent upon the Count for the success of their scheme. As their feudal overlord, they must look to him for justice, and therefore Marcellina must put her case before him.

In this scene, the two opposing camps are openly at war upon the stage. The producer's task is to translate their motives, their thoughts and their words into their actions, and by his grouping of the characters to underline the conflict between them. If, as is so often done, the producer lines up the characters in front of the footlights, they can only sing their words to the audience, and the point is lost. At Glyndebourne, Professor Ebert sets the characters in a diagonal across the stage. At the back are Bartolo, Marcellina and Basilio, in the middle, the Count, and in front, Figaro, Susanna and the Countess.

In this way the position of all the parties is at once

CEDAR CREST COLLEGE
LIBRARY

made clear. Bartolo and his friends are then singing their words and directing their hatred through the Count at Figaro and Susanna. When she refers to the bond Marcellina can point at Figaro. The Count forms a sort of bridge, over which Marcellina's complaints can alone reach their destination.

The Count, in the middle, is, of course, biased in favour of Marcellina, because in her he sees the only way of preventing the otherwise inevitable marriage of Figaro. From his position on the stage, his attitude in the matter is made clear, for he turns his back for the most part on Marcellina, and thus seems to join with her in her assault upon Figaro.

In the front of the stage, Figaro, Susanna and the Countess are taken up with themselves, and with considering how they can answer the attacks of the others. Their words are spoken to each other, and it is therefore right that they should be huddled together in a frightened group in front of the stage, looking to each other for protection. For the moment they are the target for the stones the others are throwing at them over the Count's head.

Musically this Finale is certainly the most remarkable to be found in any of Mozart's operas. It is the supreme example of the conventional Italian *opera finale* of the period, in which all the characters appeared, one after the other, until the whole cast was assembled. This was the convention, but in Mozart's hands it ceases to be a mere convention. Credit is also due to Da Ponte, for the dramatic interest is built up in such a way as to enable the characters to converge without detracting from the plot. In an often-quoted passage in his *Memoirs*,[1] he gives an amusing description of this type of finale. For a detailed

[1] Vol. I, page 97.

account of this subject, however, the reader is referred to Dent[1] and to Jahn.[2]

ACT III

This Act culminates with the wedding procession, and the question has at once to be considered whether the whole Act should be played in one scene, as is often done, or whether there should be two scenes. At first sight there appear to be several insuperable obstacles in the way of the second alternative. Firstly, there is little time to change the scenery, for the wedding march at the beginning of Scene 2 starts up before the characters have left the stage at the end of Scene 1. Secondly, a considerable amount of space is required for the first part of the Act, so that a mere drop curtain in front would not provide enough room. Thirdly, the first scene must at once be a passage and a room. A passage, because all the characters in turn pass in and out in a manner which would seem unreal in a vast room, where the wedding is later to take place. A room, because there must be a table at which Susanna writes the letter, and enough space for Barbarina and her maidens to present their bouquets. On looking more closely at the music of the wedding march—for it is here that the scene must be changed if at all—it will be seen that there is a short interval of about twenty bars for the change. At Glyndebourne the first scene of the Act is set in front of a panelled wall. The table stands in front of the wall, and on either side are doorways with curtains drawn aside. Behind, as the scene draws to its end, the lights of the wedding-room, which is already mounted, can be seen. The stage appears to represent the ante-room, in the nature of a passage. The wedding-room is set up in

[1] Page 154.   [2] Vol. II, page 324.

readiness behind, with the chorus and bridesmaids in position. When the brief moment arrives, all that remains to be done is to remove the wall and table and reveal the procession making its way across the stage.

At the beginning of the Act the Count is half sitting on the table, and does not notice the Countess, in the doorway on the right, sending Susanna in to make her rendezvous with him. For their duet, the Count and Susanna should stand close together, he trying to embrace her, and she escaping each time from his advances. As she goes out, she speaks to Figaro in the doorway without his being seen by the Count. His aria, which follows, is an epitome of his character. Unimaginative and consequently cruel, he is blindly jealous of his servant's happiness.

In Beaumarchais' play, the trial of Marcellina's action against Figaro takes place on the stage. This trial scene is one of the political elements of the play; on the surface it is an amusing burlesque of the law, but underneath it is a bitter and probably by no means exaggerated account of the ordinary administration of justice. Mozart and Da Ponte had no reason to repeat this unmasking of the humbug of the law in their opera, and the trial is left out. Trials on the stage are seldom impressive, if only because processes which may take days to complete have to be telescoped and fitted into a few moments. Beaumarchais had a definite political purpose in including the trial, but Da Ponte makes it take place off the stage. There was a preliminary hearing of the action at the end of Act II, and the ground was thus prepared for the entry of Curzio, the Judge, announcing his decision that Figaro must pay Marcellina her debt, or marry her. This latter he cannot do without the consent of his parents, and so comes the great Sextet, when Bartolo and Marcellina acknowledge him as their long-lost son. For this Sextet the comparative narrowness of the scene is a great asset. All the characters are lined up, and Figaro, and later Susanna, passes down the line embracing his parents in turn.

At this point, there is nothing apparently to prevent the wedding being celebrated at once. But there are various matters which must first be cleared up, some of them in preparation for the next Act, but most of them merely to round off the fate of the odd characters in the drama. From the point of view of construction this is the weakest point in the opera. Here is a sequence of no less than five short scenes, all of them necessary links in the story. The suggestion of a passage in the Glyndebourne setting obviates many of the difficulties, and the two doorways are convenient for the various off-stage asides.

When the wedding march finally strikes up, the scene is quickly changed, and the stage set for the wedding scene. At Glyndebourne this scene makes the most ingenious use of three different levels. On top is a flying bridge from which the general chorus can watch the proceedings. Next, there is a flat stage at the top of the steps upon which the Fandango is danced, and then at the bottom are two chairs, one on each side for the Count and Countess, who sit opposite each other. If they are set side by side, it is impossible for Susanna effectively to slip her note into the Count's hand. If, on the other hand, as here, the bridal pairs come down the steps together, then divide, the female to receive her crown from the Count and the male a buttonhole from the Countess, then Susanna can pass the note to the Count in the sight of the whole audience, without being observed by Figaro. The ceremony over, the two couples mount the steps to watch the Fandango. Figaro leans over the balustrade and observes

the Count fumbling with the pin which sealed the note—
a necessary preparation for the events of the next Act.

ACT IV

The intrigue which has gone before, although complicated enough, is nothing compared with what takes place
in the Garden. This last Act is a long series of involved
events, a grim game of charades, of which every move
must be understood by the audience. On the stage, the
different characters must remain hidden from one another,
and virtually indistinguishable. The setting of the scene
is therefore all-important.

At Glyndebourne the stage is on two different levels,
joined by a central flight of steps. At the back, on the
left, is the way leading to the Castle. Opposite is a
rotunda, into which the Count eventually leads his wife,
under the impression that she is Susanna. At the top of
the steps is a garden seat, which is invaluable for the duet
between Figaro and Susanna. On each side of the steps,
surmounting the balustrade, is a little figure of a cherub.
On the lower level, on either side, are two more rotundas
—useful hiding-places—and two more seats. Thus the
space at the top of the steps is the central point of the
stage, and it is here that each principal event takes place.
Each character moves to this spot when he or she for the
moment dominates the scene. Those in hiding are placed
on either side below the steps, or in the lower rotundas,
co-spectators with the audience of what is proceeding in
the middle. The main attention of the producer is directed
to creating, at each moment, a beautiful picture. This
scenery provides the frame, in the centre of which each
event is enacted.

It is night, so that the stage must be dark—so dark,

indeed, as to lend probability to the mistaken identity of the Countess and Susanna, which is the foundation of the plot. On the other hand, the audience must be able to recognize the different characters, and at various moments, for Susanna's Rose aria in particular, the stage must be fairly light. All these variations of light are natural to a cloudy, bright moonlight night. The moon can be used somewhat irresponsibly, and made to appear and disappear as required.

The Act begins with Barbarina's only song. It seems a pity to cut this page of music, as is often done, for it is not a mere formal aria. She is looking for the pin, which sealed the Count's letter. Mozart has found the style of music exactly appropriate to this simple-minded girl, and a bare three minutes in point of time is to be gained by cutting it.

The arias of Marcellina and Basilio are in a different category altogether. Neither of these adds anything to the plot, nor to the unfolding of the characters of their singers. Marcellina sings in a rather futile manner of the ingratitude of men, whose only return for the love of women is cruelty and suspicion. The music is commonplace, and from the technical point of view the range of the aria is outside the capabilities of an ordinary contralto singer. The words of Basilio's aria are just as weak. He tells of a donkey-skin cloak, which protects him from danger, and how patience and wisdom have come to him with experience of the world. This assertion is not consistent with his behaviour throughout the opera. Both these arias were inserted to give their respective singers their just portion of one aria each. At Glyndebourne Marcellina's aria is left out, but Basilio's, which is far more interesting musically, is retained.

On the other hand, Figaro's recitative and aria are an essential part of the drama, and there is no excuse whatever for leaving them out, as is done in some productions. Here he gives free vent to his embittered feelings. On the face of it he has ample ground for suspecting Susanna, and she leads him on in order to teach him a severe lesson for even thinking of doubting her honesty. Figaro, for the moment, is a broken man. His hopes have been dashed. In Beaumarchais' play, Figaro delivers himself of a fierce political tirade at this juncture, but Da Ponte has transformed his sentiments into a personal expression of feelings. When he has finished, Figaro retires into the rotunda on the left.

For her lovely Rose aria, Susanna is at the top of the steps, in the very centre of the stage. She has been warned by Marcellina of Figaro's presence, and therefore she throws back the Countess's cloak, which she is wearing, so that he may see her. This aria is her first and only soliloquy. Until now she has never expressed her real feelings for Figaro, although her genuine love for him has been apparent enough. Now, in this utterly simple aria, she gives herself up to the contemplation of the sacred moment when he will be hers for ever. She says that she will place a crown upon her lover's head, and added point is given to the words of her song when, at the end, she places her bridal crown on the head of one of the cherubs.

For all its apparent simplicity, the aria has a double meaning. Susanna sings it at Figaro, knowing that he will misinterpret it, and think that she is referring to her meeting with the Count. Her treatment of Figaro over the whole of this episode in the story is absolutely merciless. It would have been an easy matter for her to apprise him of the plan to trap the Count, and so save Figaro from all his jealous wrath. Susanna is more discerning than

Figaro, and knows that in due course he will get over his anger, and recover his mental balance. His jealousy has earned him this treatment and he will be a wiser man at the end of it.

The preliminaries are now concluded, and the real business of the Act begins. Figaro hides on the left, and Susanna on the right, below the steps. The Countess now takes the centre of the stage, disguised as Susanna. She has braced herself to the effort, and is ready to play her part in the scheme to defeat her husband. She is at first disturbed by Cherubino, but is soon led off by her husband, who has taken the bait, and freely makes love to his wife, under the impression that she is Susanna.

Now comes the great duet between Figaro and Susanna, the climax of the complicated intrigue. Figaro has not seen Susanna hide, and he is under the impression that she has gone off with the Count. His despair has now turned to sarcasm, and his disillusionment is such that he is prepared to be an eyewitness of his wife's infidelity. Susanna calls to him and, disguising her voice, invites him to make love to her. She is putting his love for her to yet another test, and is anxious to see whether he will descend to flirting with the Countess. Luckily for him, however, he detects her identity in time, and now it is for Figaro to turn the tables upon her. He makes violent love to her, she still believing that she has succeeded in passing herself off as the Countess. This double dealing is soon over, and Figaro and Susanna quickly compose themselves, and explain all that has passed. Mozart has drawn their characters with the utmost subtlety in the music of this duet. When pretending to be the Countess, Susanna adopts a pompous vocal line wholly different from her other music. Figaro, when making love to the "Countess," assumes an exaggeratedly aristocratic mode of expression. As soon as the knot is untied, they resume their normal musical speech. This superb delicacy of character-drawing reaches its zenith in *Così fan Tutte*.

During their duet Figaro and Susanna remain at the top of the steps. On the return of the Count, Susanna disguises herself again, and Figaro is kneeling at her feet passionately declaring his love for the apparent Countess. The Count summons the Company to bear witness to his wife's infidelity, but is brought to his knees when he discovers the truth. There are tears in his eyes as he implores his wife for forgiveness. This is the supreme moment of the drama, the triumph of justice and truth over tyranny and prejudice. The lord and master is humbled, and for the first time showing himself capable of any genuine feeling and emotion. Here is not merely the satisfactory winding up of a drama, but a sign of the times, an element in the great wave of enlightenment which overthrew the tyranny of the aristocracy.

II

DON GIOVANNI

DON GIOVANNI

or "Il dissoluto punito"
(The libertine punished)

Dramma giocoso in Two Acts, by Lorenzo da Ponte

Don Giovanni, extremely licentious young
    nobleman . . . . . . Baritone
Donna Anna, engaged to be married to . Soprano
Don Ottavio . . . . . . Tenor
Commendatore . . . . . Bass
Donna Elvira, a lady from Burgos, aban-
    doned by Don Giovanni . . . Soprano
Leporello, servant to Don Giovanni . . Bass
Masetto, lover of . . . . . Baritone
Zerlina, peasant girl . . . . Soprano

The scene is laid in a town in Spain.

The above is a translation of the list of characters
which was given on the occasion of the first performance of the opera at Prague on October 29th, 1787.

SYNOPSIS OF THE STORY[1]

ACT I

Scene 1. *A Garden. Night*

Leporello keeps guard in front of Anna's house, while his
master is engaged inside. Don Giovanni, hiding his face in his

[1] The division of scenes, and the scenic directions given in this chapter,
are those that appear in the Prague and Vienna librettos.

cloak, emerges from the house. He is closely followed by Anna, who tries to hold him back and calls for help. As soon as his master appears, Leporello hides. In response to his daughter's cries the Commendatore comes out of the house, and Anna hurries off. Don Giovanni kills the Commendatore, and escapes with Leporello. Anna returns with Ottavio, only to find that her father has been murdered. She exacts a solemn oath from Ottavio that he will avenge her father's death.

Scene 2. *A Street. Night*

Leporello unsuccessfully attempts to upbraid his master about his manner of life, but Don Giovanni is even now in search of new fields of conquest. What is his disappointment when he offers his help to an apparently forlorn female, only to discover that it is Elvira, who claims to be his wife, and who has pursued him from Burgos. Don Giovanni leaves her to the tender mercies of Leporello, who shows her his wonderful catalogue of his master's conquests.

In the next episode Masetto and Zerlina are celebrating their wedding with a party of their peasant friends. Don Giovanni disturbs their revels and picks out Zerlina as his next victim. Leporello is instructed to take the rest of the party, including the irate Masetto, off to his master's house to continue their festivities. Don Giovanni's seduction of Zerlina is disturbed by the arrival of Elvira, who takes Zerlina under her wing and leads her away.

Now come Anna and Ottavio, in all ignorance, to enlist Don Giovanni's help in tracing the murderer of the Commendatore. Don Giovanni's gallant offers of help are interrupted by Elvira, who hysterically warns Anna and Ottavio against the traitor. Don Giovanni can only protest that she is mad, and takes his leave of Anna to accompany Elvira upon her way. The manner of his leave-taking reveals to Anna that he is her father's murderer, and she recounts to Ottavio the events of that terrible night. When she has gone, Ottavio determines to obtain further proof of Don Giovanni's identity.

Don Giovanni compares notes with Leporello on what has taken place since they last met.

DON GIOVANNI

Scene 3. *A Garden with two Gates locked on the outside*

In the garden Zerlina appeases Masetto as best she may. The servants appear from the house inviting the peasants to the ball. Hearing Don Giovanni approach, Masetto hides, but is discovered in time by Don Giovanni, who thus narrowly escapes compromising himself again with Zerlina. He leads them both into the house. Now appear Anna, Elvira and Ottavio, masked, who have come to attend the festivities in order to establish Don Giovanni's guilt. They are invited to the ball by Leporello. Before going into the house they solemnly pray for heaven's assistance in their mission of vengeance.

Scene 4. *A Hall, lit up and prepared for a Grand Ball*

The dance has just stopped, and Don Giovanni and Leporello invite the guests to refresh themselves. The masked guests enter, and the dance is resumed. Don Giovanni succeeds in leading Zerlina away, but her cry for help from an inner room is the signal for general confusion. Don Giovanni pretends that Leporello is the culprit, but he does not succeed in disguising the truth in this way. The masked guests reveal their identity, and accuse Don Giovanni of the murder of the Commendatore. Don Giovanni is compelled to make his escape as best he may in face of Ottavio, who draws his pistol to attack him.

ACT II

Scene 1. *A Street*

Leporello determines to leave his master, but is bribed to remain. Don Giovanni has decided to seduce Elvira's maid, and for this purpose he changes clothes with Leporello. Standing behind Leporello, he serenades Elvira, who comes down from the balcony and goes off with Leporello. Don Giovanni now serenades the maid, but he is interrupted by Masetto, who arrives with a party of peasants. They are pursuing Don Giovanni, and the latter, of course still disguised as Leporello, sends them off in different directions, and then proceeds to give Masetto a sound beating. Zerlina now comes to comfort her dejected husband.

63

Scene 2. *Dark Courtyard of Donna Anna's House, with three Doorways*

Leporello is vainly trying to escape from Elvira. He tries each doorway in turn, only to be met by Ottavio and Anna, and then by Masetto and Zerlina. He is still in his master's clothes, and is consequently surrounded by the rest of the company, who protest that he must die. As a last resort, Leporello throws off his disguise. Even this does not free him from attack. Masetto is out for revenge for his beating, and Elvira is furious for being deceived. However, Leporello makes good his escape. Ottavio now at last expresses his conviction that Don Giovanni is the murderer, and decides to refer the matter to the appropriate authority!

Scene 3. *Enclosed Space in the form of a Cemetery. Various Equestrian Statues : Statue of the Commendatore*

Leporello and Don Giovanni are ribaldly joking about their adventures, when they are sharply rebuked for their laughter by the Statue of the Commendatore. Leporello is terrified, but his nonchalant master instructs him to invite the Statue to supper, which invitation is accepted.

Scene 4. *Dark Room*

Once again Ottavio comforts Anna in her sorrow, and suggests that she should forget her grief and marry him.

Scene 5. *A Hall. A Table prepared for a Meal*

Don Giovanni at supper is interrupted by Elvira, who makes a last appeal to him to abandon his life of sin and return to her. Her entreaty is in vain, and as she goes out she sees the Statue approaching. The Statue now comes in, and reminds Don Giovanni of his invitation, and of its acceptance. He calls upon the profligate to repent, but as he will not, he is cast down into hell. The other characters assemble, and are told by Leporello of the dreadful fate of his master.

THE OPERA

Don Giovanni is widely known and appreciated for its music, but in many people's minds the music is hampered by its association with a silly and unconvincing story. It has come to be accepted that in this, as in other Mozart operas, the story does not make sense, the characters are unreal, and generally that a nonsensical slapstick comedy is worth enduring for the sake of the music.

This attitude must be my apology for adding to the vast literature on the subject of *Don Giovanni*. In this chapter I shall seek to show that it is possible, and indeed easy, to make the opera convincing on the stage. To achieve this many problems require solution, but when the text of the opera, the scenic directions[1] and the circumstances of the original productions are studied, many of these problems disappear. If a tradition of performing *Don Giovanni* on sound lines were once established, the music would be able to be appreciated because of, rather than in spite of, its association with the story.

The earlier opera, *Le Nozze di Figaro*, had been given with great success by a small Italian company at Prague, and consequently Bondini, the manager, commissioned a new opera from Mozart for the winter season of 1787. The story of *Don Juan*, which Da Ponte suggested as the subject, was nothing new. It is supposed to have originated in Spain in the early seventeenth century, and

---

[1] For the scenic directions given in the Prague and Vienna librettos I have consulted Sonnleithner's reprint (*see* Bibliography), kindly lent to me by Mr. Paul Hirsch. For the opera itself I have used the miniature Full Score edition, edited by Alfred Einstein, published by Ernst Eulenberg, Leipzig.

had been treated in all manner of ways before Mozart and Da Ponte approached it: its life has not come to an end with their version.

Mozart and Da Ponte have puzzled commentators with the title *dramma giocoso*[1] (literally "jocular drama"), which they gave to their opera. This description has led to lengthy discussion as to its true nature, and there has been much searching of heart as to whether it is properly to be classified as a tragedy or a comedy or what not. A certain amount of this discussion arose from the omission of the final sextet at the first Vienna performance of the opera in 1788. After the descent of Don Giovanni into hell, the other characters appear and glibly point the moral, *Questo è il fin di chi fa mal*—("Such is the fate of the evildoer").

As a result of its omission by Mozart himself, this sextet was often left out of performances of the opera in the nineteenth century. At the present day the better view is that the sextet should be restored to its place. The dramatic effect of ending with Don Giovanni's death might be to make the opera a tragedy, for it was thus possible to take the view that the terrible end of the hero was some-

---

[1] Professor Edward J. Dent writes: "The author, like some other English critics, seems to imagine that *Don Giovanni* is the only opera that was ever described by the title *dramma giocoso,* and that it implies something something uniquely peculiar. This is not the case. Most of the Italian comic operas of the second half of the eighteenth century are called *dramma giocosa* on the title-pages of their librettos. The Neapolitan comic operas were generally called *commedia in musica.* The word *opera* was used colloquially in the sense of musical drama as early as 1644 (Evelyn's *Diary*), and it was used in France and England as the regular name for musical drama; but *opera,* as far as I have been able to trace it, was never used on an Italian title-page until about 1860, and is rare even now. The classical Italian word is *dramma per musica* or *melodramma*; in the nineteenth century we sometimes find *tragedia lirica* (obviously taken from the old French *tragédie lyrique*) and *commedia lirica.*"

thing to be mourned. The sextet restores the balance, and makes it clear that such was not the authors' intention. They bring back the other characters, showing that the world has survived the eclipse of Don Giovanni, and that he has not brought down the universe as well as himself. On the face of it the opera is a moral tale, a solemn warning to all who aspire to follow in the steps of the evildoer. In effect it is very far from being anything of the sort. Originally, bearing in mind the mentality created by the Inquisition, the moral was probably real enough, but long before Mozart's day the idea of a visit from another world was sufficiently unreal not to be taken too seriously. Mozart and Da Ponte cannot have hoped that their opera would prove a valuable factor in the prevention of evil living! All that concerned them was to present, in new garb, a story which was popular and already widely known. Each generation produces its own versions of such familiar themes, rearranged to be up-to-date and in conformity with the current fashion. Such was also Mozart's *Don Giovanni*, the age-old moral tale, presented with a subtle note of cynicism to suit the taste of the time.

It is, of course, in no sense an *opera seria*, neither is it an *opera buffa* or the authors would so have called it.[1] The opera must not be taken in the heavy romantic manner that was the custom in the nineteenth century, but a balance must be struck between this and pure comedy, for it is both by turns.

Why, then, has the story survived, and what is the reason for the continuing urge to re-furbish and re-present it? Morality has nothing to do with it, for the value of

---

[1] Prof. Dent writes: "The authors probably *would* have called it an *opera buffa* in conversation, because *opera buffa* and *dramma giocoso* mean exactly the same thing."

the story's moral is outweighed a thousandfold by its potential evil suggestive influence. No doubt the women, even of to-day, find Don Giovanni irresistible. In Elvira's place would they pursue him too? This is not all: Don Giovanni has a certain charm for the men. Are they not jealous of his success; envious of his winning manner? In their own ordinary lives, whether in their city office or country mansion, they know that they have not his daring. Their existence is plain and drab; his glamorous and thrilling. The supernatural side of the story also has its interest, appealing to romantics of every generation. The Commendatore is just an ordinary nobleman, but his Statue's intervention is awe-inspiring. And those trombones that accompany the Statue's utterances; have they not still the power to excite, and even frighten? The fact is that for all the hard-bitten outlook of the modern world, the appearances of the Statue continue to send a cold shiver down the back. The whole conception is outside the ordinary experience of life, and in spite of its unreality, it is none the less gripping.

Of Mozart's version, apart from the music, neither the construction of the piece nor the character-drawing stand close examination. The opera was produced in great haste, Da Ponte taking his libretto in large measure from Bertati's libretto for *Il Convitato di pietra*, an opera on the same subject, with music by Gazzaniga, that had recently appeared. Da Ponte and Mozart strung their scenes together without great regard for geography or chronology, leaving a legacy of inconsistencies and difficulties with which producers have had to grapple ever since. Into this hastily compiled framework Mozart poured his immortal music, in face of which the imperfections of the other elements of the scheme are forgotten or willingly endured. Regarded

from the purely formal point of view, *Don Giovanni* is a
thoroughly unsatisfactory piece of work. It has no continuity, no symmetry, and none of the beauty of form of,
for example, *Così fan Tutte*. All the same, there is often
something more fascinating about a work of art that
grapples with some vast problem and yet fails to solve it
satisfactorily. Perfect beauty defies analysis and silences
criticism. The work that just fails in its object inspires
effort and incites renewed attempts to make it perfect. So
it is with *Don Giovanni*.

THE CHARACTERS

Leporello is the central figure of the opera. In the fantastic world in which it is played, he is the one real person,
the firm rock of reality in the midst of a dream. He is the
reasonable man, the man on the Clapham omnibus, as
Lord Justice Bowen put it. If the audience is too prone to
be carried away by Don Giovanni's gallantry or by Elvira's
misery, it is Leporello who brings it back to earth. The
whole opera may be regarded as Leporello's dream; where
in a real world would such figures appear as Don Giovanni
or the Statue? He goes through the most extraordinary
experiences for the sake of his master, never questioning
the latter's authority to others, only grumbling to himself
or to Don Giovanni. He is ready to deal with each situation as it arises, coping in turn with an irate husband, a
deserted wife, a dead man's statue, and he even survives
the shock of witnessing Don Giovanni's descent into Hell.
Through each of these experiences his reactions are those of
the normal man. He is genuinely terrified by the Statue,
for instance, and quails beneath the table in the presence of
Hell! At the end, however, he throws off the past with-

out any difficulty. He has not suffered by his master's downfall, and even hell fire has not left him a nervous wreck. Having recounted the details of Don Giovanni's end to the others, he picks up his bag and announces his intention of finding a new master. The whole thing was a dream. He is too sane to let it affect him deeply. Leporello is almost the hero. The opera rests more on his shoulders than on those of his master.

Don Giovanni himself is the reckless libertine, who has brought dangerous living to a fine art, and absolutely refuses to know the meaning of fear until actually faced with death. What is his motive for pursuing women? It must be something more than mere physical lust. Perhaps it is ambition, or the insatiable desire to conquer new fields, or the thrill of adventure. It seems strange that his enthusiasm should have survived the number of conquests recorded in Leporello's catalogue. Will he never be disillusioned, never tired? Will he always imagine that his newest adventure will be more thrilling than any previous one? Ambition and pride probably more truly represent his motives. He has never yet failed to subject a woman by his charms, and admission of failure in any given case would be a recognition of the approach of middle age, the waning of his star. There is apparently no question of social ambition. All types of women are potential conquests. He flouts conventions and defies the institutions of an ordered life. His dreadful end is the victory of stable society over one who will not conform to its standards. That is why the story is immortal, for the conflict between society and the individual occurs in all ages. He who sets himself against society and its conventions will always go under in the end. This is the fate of Don Giovanni. The rules and institutions of society are too strong even for him, and since he will not conform to them, there is no place for him in the world.

Apart from Leporello, the other normal person among the men of the opera is Masetto. He is an honest peasant and sees through Don Giovanni's attempts to seduce his bride, but is ready enough to forgive her afterwards. Who would not forgive such a charming person, particularly as her affair with Don Giovanni does not survive their first encounter? Masetto has often been made to appear as a complete clown, but his music shows that he has great strength of character. He may be simple, but he is no mere fool, or he would offer no resistance to Don Giovanni. It is interesting to note that Masetto's aria in Act I, "Ho capito," was apparently the last part of the score to be written before the Prague performance. In his introduction to the score, Einstein refers to the different parts of the opera that were written by Mozart in Vienna before he arrived at Prague, and suggests that he was able to write most of the opera in advance because he knew, from his visit in February 1787, the singers who would take part. Einstein suggests that the only one whom he did not know was Giuseppe Lolli, who doubled the parts of the Commendatore and of Masetto. Hence the aria was left to the end until he knew his singer. It is also possible that Mozart may have wished to strengthen the part of Masetto by making him resist Don Giovanni's brutality, and added the aria for this purpose.

Ottavio is the most difficult of the men; he has to sing the formal music of a leading lyric tenor, and behave as a spineless operatic hero. He scarcely seems to come to life throughout the opera, but some attempt must be made to turn him into a convincing character. E. T. A. Hoffmann has some valuable suggestions to make in his fanciful story

Don Juan.[1] At one stage in his career, in 1808, Hoffmann became musical director in Bamberg, where the inn "Zur Rose" was connected with the theatre by a private entrance to one of the boxes. Hoffmann's story tells of a visitor to the inn who attends a performance of the opera in the adjoining theatre. After the performance he returns to the theatre, and sits in the box writing a letter to a friend. The letter contains Hoffmann's own interpretation of the opera. It is a romantic interpretation, and as such has been freely criticized, but his observations on some of the characters are useful. His description of Ottavio is worth reproducing:

> A tender, well-groomed dandy, at the most twenty-one years of age. As Anna's betrothed he can be called up so quickly because he probably lives in the house[2]; at the first cry, which he certainly must have heard, he could have hurried out and saved her father; but he has to tidy himself, and is reluctant to be called out in the night at all.

The character of Anna presents many difficulties. Although infused with great fire and determination, her music is essentially typical of a dramatic soprano. She is scarcely human, and even when her father's murder has been satisfactorily avenged, she insists on waiting a year before considering Ottavio's suit. Here again, Hoffmann is illuminating. He has come in for a lot of criticism because he assumes, as the basis of his remarks about Anna, that she was actually seduced by Don Giovanni. From the text there is nothing to justify this assumption, and many writers have taken upon themselves the task of defending Anna's honour against Hoffmann's charges!

[1] *See* Bibliography.   [2] Of this more later!

John Brownlee as THE DON in *Don Giovanni*
(Glyndebourne)

His thesis, which certainly makes Anna's motives psychologically real, can stand just as well without the seduction. His idea is that Anna, a voluptuous woman at heart, has been roused for the first and only time in her life by Don Giovanni. He alone could awaken her dormant passion, and beside him, the great romantic lover, her own Ottavio cuts a poor figure. Before Don Giovanni appeared, she knew no better than to believe that she loved Ottavio; but once awakened to the greater overpowering passion which she feels for Don Giovanni, all else fades. "She feels that only Don Giovanni's end can bring peace to her tortured spirit; but this peace is her own earthly end." It follows from this, as Hoffmann points out, that she will never marry Ottavio.

The same passion consumed Elvira, though she alone succeeded in marrying Don Giovanni. He has deserted her, and moved by the same overwhelming thirst for his downfall, she warns the world of his infamy. Jealousy is her real motive. No one else shall have him, if she may not. Such conduct is a thin disguise. She is still desperately in love with the man, and would take him back to-morrow if he would come; but knowing that she can no longer hold him she determines that no one else shall take her place. If Anna is the lady, the nobleman's daughter, Elvira belongs to the middle class. She had great beauty in her day, but once cast aside, all poise is gone, and her natural character reveals itself. She behaves like any other disappointed parvenue, and Leporello's aside,—*Pare un libro stampato* ("She's like a printed book")—sums her up, for she is essentially the bore of the opera. She continually pursues Don Giovanni, for ever reminding him that she is his wife. In a sense she is the only one who has defeated him. In order to conquer her, he had to satisfy her middle-class outlook by going through some form of marriage with her! She never ceases to "nag" at him, and her music is all in the same tragic vein. A healthy sense of humour would have stood her in good stead. Apart from Don Giovanni she has no status in the world, and unless she can establish her claim to be his wife she has no reason to live.

A tradition seems to have grown up that Anna, and not Elvira, is the principal lady in the opera. The *prima donna* of the opera company is usually cast as Anna, and Elvira is left to a singer of less experience. But the claims of both parts, from the musical point of view, are equal, and Elvira is surely the more difficult part to act. A fine actress can make little of the part of Anna however hard she tries, but her experience and technique can find ample scope in the part of Elvira.

Zerlina is the most normal woman of the opera. She is not a coquette, nor an inexperienced country girl. Don Giovanni is not the first man with whom she has had to deal, nor the first of the aristocracy who has paid attention to her. But she has never before been handled with such deference, or treated as an equal by one of them. In the normal run of things, Masetto, as the peasant husband, would have to swallow such attentions as part of the lot of all men in his position. But after her first encounter with Don Giovanni, Zerlina has had enough of him. Not because of anything which she has been told by Elvira, but because she realizes that the glamour of that first meeting will not last and that her real happiness in life is to be found with Masetto. She does not, like the others, allow Don Giovanni to ruin her whole life, for she is endowed with a fuller measure of common sense.

THE PRODUCTION

A production of *Don Giovanni* must aim not merely at good presentation of Mozart's music, but at making the opera as a whole convincing to the modern audience. The chief difficulties in the way of this latter object are those of scenery and settings. Owing to the loose construction of the opera it is essential to maintain continuity, otherwise it deteriorates into a series of disjointed episodes. Everything must be sacrificed to speed, for long intervals for scene-changing cannot be tolerated. Nearly every scene has its own problems either arising from the interpretation of the stage directions, or as to the best arrangement of the scenery. At first sight it may seem pedantic to refer to stage directions in dealing with a work such as this, and to suggest that the original directions should be followed. Producers feel themselves free to take liberties with the staging of the classics that they would not take with the works of living authors. It is for this reason that no two productions of *Don Giovanni*—or of any other of Mozart's operas—are in the least degree similar. This may be due to the traditions and equipment of the particular theatre, but more likely to the fancy of the producer. There are, of course, works that have survived which were written to be presented in circumstances that cannot be reproduced to-day. Such works must be adapted if they are to be given on the modern stage. In the case of *Don Giovanni*, however, the circumstances of its original production are known, and detailed directions by the authors are set out in the librettos of the first two productions. A producer may interpret these in his own way, but there is no excuse for ignoring or contradicting them. The inconsistencies that have come to be accepted as normal in productions of the opera often arise from this cause alone.

In Act I these stage directions cause considerable confusion, particularly in Scene 2, which contains five episodes apparently requiring changes of scenery. The solution of this, and the problems of the individual scenes, are considered later.

The second main difficulty arises from the fact that when the opera came to be performed at Vienna in 1788, Mozart added various numbers which do not fit into its original dramatic form. Two of these are usually retained in modern productions because of their great beauty. The first, Ottavio's "Dalla sua pace," presents no great difficulty. It is essentially a concert number, and does not add to the plot, but it fits in quite harmlessly in the place in which it was intended to be sung. The second addition was to Scene 2 of Act II, where after Ottavio's "Il mio tesoro" (which was left out of the Vienna performance), Mozart added a duet for Zerlina and Leporello, and a recitative and aria for Elvira. The problems which arise out of these additions to the opera will be discussed later.

A third point to remember is that *Don Giovanni* was written for a particular company, and designed to suit their individual resources. For instance the music on the stage in the supper scene at the end of the opera is written for wind instruments only, because Bondini's company happened to possess exceptional talent in this department. On the other hand no chorus in the proper sense was available. Bondini's company consisted solely of a few singers, and he probably had not the funds to engage a chorus. For this reason the only choruses in the opera are the chorus of peasants in the wedding scene, and the chorus of demons which accompanies Don Giovanni's descent into hell at the

end of the opera. In addition, there is a small chorus of
four servants who issue the invitation to the peasants to
come to the ball. Each of these choruses is very short, and
not in the least exacting from the musical point of view.
At the performances at Prague they were probably safely
entrusted to supernumerary singers whom Bondini could
collect together for the occasion. There is no reason to
exceed these limits in producing the opera to-day. A large
chorus is not required, and only detracts from the intimacy
of the opera, which is concerned entirely with the conduct
of the individual characters.

One word of caution about the general style of the
setting of the opera. Apart from the statement that the
"Scene is laid in a town in Spain," and that Elvira comes
from Burgos, there is nothing Spanish about this version of
the Don Juan legend. As Dent points out, Da Ponte
probably conceived the opera in terms of his native Italy
rather than against a Spanish background, and the setting
of Scene 2 of Act II seems to be conclusive proof of this.
Too many productions of *Don Giovanni* are spoiled by
elaborate Spanish costumes and settings, which give the
opera a false background.

It is noteworthy that the directions contain no hint as
to the period of the opera.

As in so many great works, the time factor does not
appear to have been thought out very carefully by the
authors. The inconsistencies of time probably pass unnoticed by any but the most meticulous member of the
audience, but it is as well to clarify the question, and the
following scheme is based on such guidance as is to be had
from the directions and from the remarks of the characters.

Act I, Scene 1.—No difficulty arises here, as the scene
begins fairly late in the evening of the first day (Day I).

The direction is "Night," and there is nothing inconsistent with this in the scene. When Anna later describes the events leading up to this scene, she says *Era già alquanto avanzata la notte* ("The night was already fairly well advanced") when Don Giovanni came into her room.

Scene 2.—The direction that covers the whole of this scene is "Night." Clearly this cannot apply to any but the first episode, and the following time-table is therefore suggested:

> Episode (*a*). Don Giovanni, Leporello and Elvira. Late evening of Day II.

The events of Scene 1 must have occupied the whole of one evening, and so it is supposed that this is the next day.

> Episode (*b*). Peasants' wedding chorus; (*c*) attempted seduction of Zerlina; (*d*) arrival of Anna and Ottavio. Afternoon of Day III.
>
> Episode (*e*). Don Giovanni and Leporello.
>
> *Scene 3.*—The garden.
>
> *Scene 4.*—The ballroom.
>
> Early evening, late evening, and night of Day III.

It is clear that all the events of Act I from Episode (*b*) of Scene 2 onwards take place on the same day. It may be assumed that the peasants' wedding chorus is in the afternoon, and that Leporello takes the peasants off to refreshments at Don Giovanni's house. They occupy the interval until the ball in the garden, where they are found in Scene 3. In Episode (*e*), after discussing the events of the afternoon, Don Giovanni looks forward to the festivities of the evening when he says *Le voglio divertir fin che vien notte* ("I'll entertain them till nightfall"). In Scene 3 the evening is already fairly far advanced, because the ballroom is prepared, and the musicians are beginning to play.

One further small point may be mentioned for the sake

of completeness. At the end of the ballroom scene the other characters sing to Don Giovanni *Sul tuo capo in questo giorno il suo fulmine cadrà* ("Before this day is ended the blow shall fall on your head"). It has been suggested that this shows that the authors contemplated the whole opera as taking place in one day! These words, however, are only a figure of speech, because it cannot be possible for the characters who sing them to forecast the events of Act II with such accuracy.

Act II. There is no great difficulty about the timing of this Act, and, for the reasons given below, the following chronology is suggested:

    Scene 1.   Early evening of Day IV.
    Scene 2.   Later, Evening of Day IV.
    Scene 3.   Night of Day IV–V.
    Scene 4.   Afternoon of Day V.
    Scene 5.   Evening of Day V.

The first scene takes place in the early evening, the direction at the beginning of the serenade to Elvira being that it is gradually getting dark. The next two scenes follow closely upon the first. In Scene 2 Leporello—still disguised in his master's clothes—continues the escapade that was begun in Scene 1.

At the beginning of Scene 3 Don Giovanni looks at his watch and remarks, *Ancor non sono due della notte,* which at first sight seems to mean that it is 2 a.m. Dent points out, however, that this more probably means two hours after dark. The invitation to the Statue is to come to supper "this evening," and if Dent is right, Scenes 4 and 5 would follow on the same night. Two difficulties are inherent in this solution. If Scene 4 is to be in Anna's house, as will be proposed later, the old controversy arises as to whether it is proper for her to receive Ottavio at such

79

a late hour. This is avoided if the scene is postponed until the next afternoon. Secondly, it was already getting dark in Scene 1, and the events since then have surely occupied more than two hours, particularly if a scene is inserted to include Elvira's aria "Mi tradì." The eeriness of the cemetery is enhanced if the time is 2 a.m., and in the popular imagination the moon is more likely to be up then than two hours after darkness! It is also strictly correct for Don Giovanni to contemplate supper with the Statue "this evening," i.e. some 18 hours later.

On balance, therefore, it is suggested that the scheme set out above is reasonable, and avoids all difficulties. Nor is it upset by the insertion of a scene to include "Mi tradì." Such a scene could be supposed to follow, in point of time, directly after Scene 2, and the adventures referred to by Masetto might, with a stretch of the imagination, be assumed to have taken place after Scene 2. Masetto describes how he saw a woman weeping and a man fleeing, and he concludes that it was Don Giovanni. The fact that this took place after Scene 2 is the more likely because at the beginning of Scene 3, Don Giovanni tells Leporello that he has been involved in just such an episode since they last met.

Apart from the fact that it precedes the supper scene, there is no clue to the timing of Scene 4, which may therefore be supposed to take place in the afternoon of Day V.

Another time factor that has caused considerable discussion is the fact that a Statue should have been erected in the cemetery to the Commendatore so soon after his death. Some critics have suggested that the Statue is one that was erected during his lifetime, but the inscription upon it and its presence in the cemetery, dispose of this theory. No solution can be found to this problem.

Audrey Mildmay as ZERLINA in *Don Giovanni*
(Glyndebourne)

ACT I

Scene 1

The indication is that this scene takes place in a garden at night, in the grounds of Anna's mansion. The curtain rises on Leporello walking up and down in a cloak keeping watch. He expresses himself in no uncertain terms about his master, but quickly hides when he hears him coming. He stays in hiding until the end of the scene, peeping out from time to time to see what is going on. Observe that Don Giovanni comes out first, struggling to free himself from Anna, and to keep his identity from her. The direction is "Donna Anna holding tight to Don Giovanni's arm" and later "Don Giovanni still trying to free himself." Presumably she is holding on to him until help arrives, when she will hand him over; and yet, as soon as she hears her father, she hurries back into the house. ("Donna Anna, hearing the Commendatore, releases Don Giovanni and goes into the house.") Why she should hurry back, instead of pointing out the villain to her father, is not clear, unless perhaps she has something of which to be ashamed. Is Hoffmann right after all? Not necessarily, for if he were, Anna would scarcely cry for help; rather would she try to get Don Giovanni back into the house unobserved, and let him out by a side door later on. Anna cannot be blamed for escaping. Whatever may have occurred, to be found by her father struggling with a strange man outside the house is not an easy situation for her. Her father at once loyally assumes that Don Giovanni is to blame, but had he lived, Anna would probably have had a difficult interview with him later on! As Rouché points out, when Anna goes back into the house she does not see any immediate peril for her father. She goes to fetch Ottavio. Whether he is in her house, or lodging nearby, does not seem to matter very much. This is a question that has troubled many commentators, who are reluctant to accept the idea that Ottavio should be in Anna's house at night. But it is not yet late, and as Anna explains later, she at first mistook Don Giovanni for Ottavio; it is clear, therefore, that she at any rate, and she is a prude, saw nothing wrong in receiving Ottavio at that time. The direction is that Anna goes into the house, but if instead she is made to go out another way and to return the same way with Ottavio, the question is left open, for this exit may lead out into the street, or into any other part of the house.

If it can be arranged, it is as well for the Commendatore to come out of the house by a different door from that used by Anna and Don Giovanni. Such a plan makes it clear that he was in another part of the house, and knew nothing of Don Giovanni's presence. As it is still early, he should not appear in night attire.

Some steps, possibly leading down from the main door of the house, are of the utmost value for the convincing staging of the duel, and particularly when the Commendatore is killed. He falls so that he is reclining on them, and can then be seen and heard during his death trio. Leporello and Don Giovanni make their escape, and Anna returns with Ottavio. Hoffmann's interpretation is certainly justified here. Ottavio, full of good intentions as long as definite action is not called for, is horrified by the whole thing. He has the presence of mind to call for some stimulant for Anna, and then orders someone else to remove the body. He himself would rather not stain his hands by touching such an *oggetto d'orrore*. It is important to note that when Anna first recovers herself, she mistakes Ottavio for her father's murderer, thus adding reality to the story she tells later. For this scene, then, Don Giovanni and Ottavio must be dressed to look as much alike as possible.

Scene 2

The direction is "Night, a Street," and no change of scenery is indicated for any of the numerous episodes that make up the scene. As has been pointed out, "Night" can only refer to the first episode, the encounter between Don Giovanni, Leporello and Elvira, and it is, of course, possible that the directions for the other scenes were never written down. In view of the detail in which the other stage directions appear in the Prague and Vienna librettos, this is unlikely. It must therefore be assumed that the authors intended this scene to be played without any change of setting. Many other schemes have been tried, according to the resources of the theatre. As an instance, the following series of scenes were mounted in the Glyndebourne production:

Episode (*a*). A street.
Episodes (*b*), (*c*) and (*d*). Garden of Don Giovanni's house.
Episode (*e*). Don Giovanni's dressing-room.

This sequence had many advantages that will be mentioned later; the main objection was that the peasants should assemble for their celebrations in a private garden! No such elaborate ideas should be adopted, however, unless the speediest possible changing of scenery can be achieved. If there is any risk of delay it is better to have one setting only, which may be a public square, possibly with an inn on one side, and Don Giovanni's house on the other. In the first episode Elvira is directed to appear in travelling clothes, and it may be assumed that she intends to put up at the inn. In this case the same set can be used for the first scene of Act II. Some producers have made Elvira arrive on the scene with all her luggage, having just come from Burgos. Discussion on this point does not seem helpful. In any case it is inadvisable for her to be accompanied by her maid in this scene, for Don Giovanni would scarcely wait until the next Act to pursue her, when once he knew of her existence. Here is Don Giovanni, the experienced libertine: *Mi pare sentir odor di femmina* ("I seem to scent a woman")—and Leporello, by comparison, the realist. His primary concern is to know the lady's name for inclusion in his catalogue—a subtle preparation for the great song to come. When Elvira appears, Leporello hides, popping out from time to time to pour cold water on his master's enthusiasm: *Così ne consolò mille e ottocento.* (There are one thousand eight hundred women whom he has "consoled" in this way!) Don Giovanni disappears, leaving Leporello to deal with Elvira. He shows her his catalogue of his master's conquests. The treatment of this aria must be left to the particular singer. Great play can be made with a book which unfolds like a panorama postcard, but on no account must there be any fumbling. This is not the first time that Leporello has displayed his masterpiece to an audience. He knows it almost by heart. It is a mistake to introduce a pair of spectacles and make him look closely at the book when it comes to the *rallentando* at the words *Ma in Ispagna,* as if he were uncertain of the figure. The *rallentando*—which, by the way, only lasts two bars—is a pause of pride. Here is the supreme page of his masterpiece, devoted, appropriately enough, to Spain.

When the aria is over there is a short recitative for Elvira, in which she says that she will take vengeance on Don Giovanni for the wrongs he has done to her. The general practice is to leave this out. It adds nothing to the plot, and is extremely difficult to fit in from the dramatic point of view. In some productions Elvira's recitative, "In quali eccessi" and aria "Mi tradì," which will be discussed later, have been sung here, but Leporello's catalogue aria is the obvious conclusion of the scene, and anything after it must be an anti-climax. Elvira should therefore walk off in disgust in the middle of the aria, leaving Leporello to finish his aria alone.

In the next episode the peasants come dancing on to the stage, leading in the bridal pair, and singing as they go. It is quite conceivable that they intend to continue their celebrations at the inn. Don Giovanni and Leporello enter from the precincts of his house. Having picked out Zerlina, Don Giovanni instructs Leporello to take the rest of the party into the house. Masetto at once sees through Don Giovanni's designs. It is bitter music that he has to sing, not the unheeding acquiescence of a fool, and it is only at the point of the sword that he is at last forced away. Now comes the question of the *casinetto,* i.e. summer house. This cannot be in the house itself, for thither Leporello has led the rest of the peasants, nor can it be somewhere off the stage, for unless she catches Don Giovanni and Zerlina actually going in at the door, Elvira has no good reason for her interference. There must therefore be two obvious entrances to Don Giovanni's house: one principal entrance, and another leading through the *casinetto* perhaps into the garden. It is here that the main difficulty of the scene arises. A public square seems very unsuitable for such delicate intimacy as occurs between

Don Giovanni and Zerlina. Hence the garden introduced at Glyndebourne. This is the only occasion in the opera when Don Giovanni is really seen as the lover. He pursues Zerlina ardently and directly, and there must be no glossing over the intimacy with which he woos her; in fact, the heat of the atmosphere should cause the audience to feel acutely embarrassed.

Just as Don Giovanni opens the door of the *casinetto*, in comes Elvira on her mission to save Zerlina. She takes Zerlina into the house to re-unite her with Masetto.

Having regard to what they say, it is clear that Anna and Ottavio have purposely called on Don Giovanni to enlist his help, and it is therefore reasonable to stage this episode in the garden of his house. On the other hand, the original street is equally appropriate. (As mourning dress for Anna and Ottavio is not mentioned here, but is specifically directed in Act II, Scene 2, it was presumably intended that they should not wear mourning in this scene. There does not seem to be any good reason for this distinction unless it be supposed that the black clothes they wear in the later scene are not yet ready!)

When Elvira returns, she takes up her position in the centre of the stage. Such is her agitation that it looks at first as though there is some truth in Don Giovanni's assertion that she is mad. Ottavio and Anna stand apart, bewildered, and Don Giovanni moves to and fro between them and Elvira, talking confidentially to each in turn. He abandons at once any idea of escape, for that would be an admission of the truth of Elvira's accusations, but he gives himself away without realizing that he has done so. Saying that he must follow Elvira to see that she comes to no harm, he takes his leave of Anna, assuring her of his readiness to assist her: *Se servirvi poss' io, in mia casa v'aspetto* ("If I can help you, I will attend upon you in my house"). Forgetting himself for a moment, he adopts the caressing tones of the trained lover for the last words, and Anna at once recognizes her father's murderer. Those few words, and the manner in which they are spoken, are a sure test of any interpretation of the part of Don Giovanni. Nothing approaching physical contact—an embrace or handshake—is necessary for his recognition, his tone of voice alone suffices to betray him. When Anna has sung her aria, Ottavio, left alone, sings the aria added for the first Vienna production, "Dalla sua pace." Rouché makes an interesting point on Ottavio's brief recitative which precedes the aria. Ottavio says, speaking of Anna, *Disingannar la voglio, o vendicarla* ("I will disillusion her, or avenge her"). That "o" is important. Ottavio, cautious as ever, and reluctant to act without proof, determines to be sure of Don Giovanni's guilt before taking steps to avenge the murder. If he finds Don Giovanni to be innocent, he will disillusion Anna; on the other hand, if guilty, he will set about seeking vengeance. Rouché points out that this uncertainty and desire for definite proof are the justification for the masks later on.

The short episode between Don Giovanni and Leporello which follows can, of course, take place in the street. There are, however, some difficulties in the way of this, which are overcome by staging the scene in the dressing-room. The conversation shows that Don Giovanni and Leporello are snatching a moment or two to compare notes on their respective adventures. Leporello reports that the peasants are already half drunk, possibly indicating that he has slipped upstairs to help his master, before returning to deal with them. He also remarks that when Elvira brought Zerlina along he got rid of the former by pushing her out into the street and locking the garden gate behind her. This has a bearing on the next scene.

Don Giovanni's aria, called the champagne aria, is clearly improved if he is holding a glass in his hand, and the dressing-room gives Leporello something to do during the aria. He can busy himself brushing his master's coat, and generally getting him ready for the ball. The whole atmosphere is one of tension and excitement.

Scene 3

There is nothing to explain the extraordinary direction for the setting of this scene, which is "A garden, with two gates locked on the outside," except the remark of Leporello referred to above. This only disposes of one gate, which Leporello locked on the inside. If both gates are locked, how do Anna, Elvira and Ottavio enter later on? The second part of the direction can conveniently be ignored, and the scene set in the garden with gates leading into the street. There must also be an entrance to the house from which the servants enter to invite the peasants to the ball, and through which the music from the ball-room can be heard. Some shrubs will suffice for Masetto to conceal himself. Observe that Zerlina is genuinely frightened at the approach of Don Giovanni, and not in the least anxious to encourage his attentions. She is immensely relieved when the music from the ballroom provides an excuse for bringing this part of the scene to an end.

When Anna, Elvira and Ottavio appear in masks[1] and

---

[1] They are masked for the simple reason that they desire to conceal their identity. The masks have no other complicated significance connected with the ball.

Professor Edward J. Dent writes: "The only reason I can see for Anna, Elvira and Ottavio wearing masks is that it was customary at Venice in

accept Leporello's invitation to the ball, it is a mistake for
them to sing their trio in front of the curtain as is done in
some productions. It is reasonable to argue that this trio
is merely the expression of the thoughts of the masked
guests, and is entirely outside the action of the opera. The
sequence of events is that the masks, having accepted the
invitation, would presumably walk straight into the house.
Their lingering in the garden during the trio would be
unreal. By making them sing it in front of the curtain,
the producer differentiates their thoughts from their
actions. But this is the most solemn music in the opera.
They are offering up a prayer for divine aid in their
mission of vengeance, and calling down the censure of
heaven upon the house of Don Giovanni. The point of
this music is lost unless it be sung in the dark garden in
front of the house.

Scene 4

The first of the many problems that arise in this scene
is the handling of the three orchestras on the stage. The
reason for them is not clear. Probably they were included
to give an effect of grandeur. Schnerich suggests that
there should be two doorways leading into other rooms at
the back of the stage. One orchestra is then on the stage
itself, and the other two are placed in the doorways but
actually playing for the rooms beyond. In principle this
procedure is sound, but its application in practice may not
be easy. The company invited to the ball is very mixed,
and the different grades of society would tend to segregate

the eighteenth century for ladies and gentlemen to go out at night wearing
what modern costumiers call 'Longhi' masks. It seems quite certain that
the first performances of *Don Giovanni* were dressed in contemporary
costume, and Da Ponte seems to have imagined a Venetian rather than a
Spanish background."

themselves from each other, and in real life, as opposed to the stage, there could well be three different rooms for dancing. On the stage, however, all the dancers must be visible to the audience. Ottavio leads off with Anna in a Minuet to the accompaniment of the first orchestra; Don Giovanni partners Zerlina in the second orchestra's less elegant Contredanse; while Leporello forces Masetto to dance the "popular" Ländler played by the third orchestra. Elvira does not dance at all. All this must be seen, and there is therefore no alternative but to have all the orchestras on the stage.

The first orchestra is the most important, comprising both wind and string players, and may conveniently occupy the centre of the back of the stage—possibly placed on a raised dais. The second and third orchestras must be disposed in the most appropriate manner, one on each side of the stage. The second orchestra may conveniently be in a raised gallery, with an entrance behind it, thus suggesting that the main body of the dancers of the Contredanse are in a room beyond. Don Giovanni may then start dancing in the main room, and gradually take Zerlina off with him through this exit. Masetto, forced to dance by Leporello, observes what is going on, and breaks away to follow Zerlina. If such a plan is adopted, the three members of the second orchestra should sit in their gallery in a semi-circle, facing towards the room beyond. The leader should be at the back, facing the conductor.

Zerlina's scream interrupts the dancing, and Don Giovanni drags in Leporello as the culprit. He pretends to try to kill him, but his sword appears to stick in its sheath. From this point onwards the action freezes. Ottavio is directed to draw a pistol, the masks reveal their identity, and a long and formal ensemble follows. Perhaps the pistol is better left out. Ottavio's indecisive conduct hitherto makes it unlikely that he would ever bring himself to fire it, and it looks silly for him to stand holding it throughout the rest of the scene. The directions are silent as to the end of the scene, the curtain apparently coming down on the assembled company. In any case there is no duel with Ottavio. Ottavio may, however, conveniently have a sword, and at the very end of the scene Don Giovanni should draw his sword, cut his way through the company, and get away before the others have had time to collect themselves.

It has already been pointed out that there is no music for a chorus in this scene. Don Giovanni has invited the peasants to his house to celebrate the wedding, but apart from the masks there are no other "elegant" guests. Ottavio and Anna dance the Minuet alone, while the peasants divide themselves between the other two dances. There is no point in the peasants singing with the soloists in the final ensemble, and after the turmoil aroused by Zerlina's screams they can conveniently fade out with the musicians, leaving the soloists alone for the final ensemble.

Act II

Scene 1

The only direction here is "A Street," and the same scenery may be used as for Scene 2 of Act I. The time is early evening, and the indication at the beginning of the serenade to Elvira that it is gradually getting darker and darker lends reality to her deception. The humour of this serenade is enhanced if Don Giovanni crouches behind Leporello and moves his arms for him. This is preferable to Don Giovanni standing underneath the window as he sings and leaving Leporello to gesticulate alone in the middle of the stage. Leporello's ill-disguised laughter is the result of tickling!

At the end of Don Giovanni's serenade to the maid, it is better for her not to appear. She has no music, and cannot come down, so that a light, or merely a movement in the window, is all that is necessary. Don Giovanni only says—*V'è gente alla finestra; forse e dessa* ("There's someone at the window, perhaps it is she"), and if the maid appeared he would scarcely be in doubt as to her identity.

The remainder of this scene is straightforward. Masetto and his party of peasants are dispersed by Don Giovanni and sent off by different routes. Their furtive steps, as they set off in pursuit of their victim, are indicated by the demi-semi-quaver figure which occurs at the beginning of Don Giovanni's song. To make sure that they go, Don Giovanni follows the peasants off the stage, returning with Masetto to give him his beating.

Scene 2

This scene has given rise to more discussion than any of the others. It has only one real purpose, which is musical and not dramatic, namely the singing of a sextet. According to the directions the scene is laid in the courtyard of Anna's house. The problem which has puzzled many producers, however, is that if this scene is laid in the precincts of a private house, how is it a public thoroughfare, where anybody and everybody can walk in and out as they please? To obviate this, many different methods of staging the scene have been suggested and tried: a cloister, a church, a subterranean passage. Anna and Ottavio, when they appear, are directed to be dressed in mourning, and it is for this reason that the precincts of a church have been chosen for the scene. They are then presumed to be just returning from prayer at the Commendatore's tomb. Sometimes, even, the scenery has included a view of a cemetery, with the statue of the Commendatore in the background. It scarcely needs to be pointed out that this anticipation detracts from the dramatic effect of the cemetery scene which follows. Dent, however, makes a practical proposal. The scene, he says, "is not, as has been supposed, a private hall in Donna Anna's house, but the usual courtyard of an Italian palace which, as we know from Goethe's *Italienische Reise*,[1] was often treated as public property." Unfortunately, of course, the ordinary member of the audience will not have read his Goethe, so that the producer's subtlety will be lost on all but the learned, and it will remain obscure why Anna's courtyard should be so public.

Leporello, still in his master's clothes, leads in Elvira, trying his best to lose her in the dark. His attempts at escape are frustrated. He tries the first door, but is interrupted by the entrance of Anna and Ottavio. At the next door he is surprised by Zerlina and Masetto, who recognize him as they meet him in the doorway. Leporello is dragged to the middle of the stage, where he crouches down in such a position that the audience, and not the

[1] The passage to which Dent presumably refers was written in Verona on September 17th, 1786, in which Goethe describes the filthy condition of the houses and streets, and the habit of the general public to make free use of the courtyards of large houses.

"The rich man may be rich, and build palaces, the nobleman may rule, but if he installs a colonnade or a courtyard, then the general public will use it for their own purposes. . . . If he does not like it, then he should not aspire to play the Grand Seigneur; in other words, he must not behave as though half his house was public property."

characters on the stage, can see his face. His only way out of the difficulty is to reveal his true identity. Once this episode is over there is no further action in this scene, except for Leporello's escape, and this is impossible to manage convincingly. Anna has retired, but the remaining four characters can do nothing better than stand by while he makes the most obvious escape. The only way to deal with this is for Leporello first to take Zerlina and Masetto to one side to assure them that it was not he who beat Masetto, and then run across to answer Ottavio's accusations, all the while getting nearer and nearer to the door at the back.

Then comes Ottavio's aria "Il mio tesoro." It is difficult to decide whether he should sing this alone, or to Elvira, Zerlina and Masetto. The words of the aria and of the recitative which precedes it make it clear beyond all reasonable doubt that Ottavio is addressing the others. He expressly says in his recitative, "My friends . . . remain in this house for a few hours," and then in the aria, "Go (plural) and console my beloved." Further, the indication at the end of the aria is "exeunt." The trouble is that it is quite impossible to find adequate employment for Elvira, Zerlina and Masetto during the aria. Dent's observations on the point are interesting. "Il mio tesoro," he says, is addressed, not to human listeners, but "to zephyrs, roses, sighs, or any other Metastasian substitute for the workaday channels of information." "It is hardly likely," he goes on, "that at such a very late hour of the night Ottavio would have invited two peasants and a strange lady with a tarnished reputation to spend a few hours in inflicting their consolations upon Anna." It is equally possible for Ottavio to address his remarks, in a purely general way, to the audience.

DON GIOVANNI

This issue has, however, been complicated by the additions which Mozart made to the opera for the Vienna production.   In the hitherto accepted version of these additions, Zerlina drags Leporello on to the stage by the hair, threatening him with a razor, and eventually ties him to a chair.   She then goes away and in her absence Leporello frees himself, and escapes.   Zerlina returns with Elvira to show her what she has done, only to find that Leporello has gone.   Elvira assumes that Don Giovanni has helped him to escape and expresses her indignation in a recitative and aria "Mi tradì."   Meanwhile Zerlina goes off to inform Ottavio of Leporello's escape.   Presumably this whole episode was intended as a scene by itself, to be played separately from the preceding scene in Anna's courtyard.   However, the episode between Zerlina and Leporello has come to be left out, and only Elvira's recitative and aria have kept their place in performance.   As already mentioned, this music has often been fitted into Act I, after the catalogue song, so little connection with the plot does it seem to have.   Usually, however, it is sung after Ottavio's aria, during which Elvira, Zerlina and Masetto remain on the stage.   In this case it is reasonable for them to do so, as otherwise Elvira would have to return at the end to sing her music.   "Mi tradì" is the cause of the dilemma.   There need be no second thoughts about leaving out the Zerlina-Leporello duet, which is cheap, and altogether below the level of the rest of the opera.   Purely comic business, which is all that this scene amounts to, is out of place, and the music does not redeem it.   Einstein says, "It seems unlikely that this duet can ever have been sung since the performances of 1788, except . . . at the Prague performances of 1801."   Further than this, the scene provides no dramatic reason for Elvira's outburst which follows it. For the sake of hearing "Mi tradì," how-ever, it is worth enduring a certain dramatic ineffectiveness.

The whole of this question has recently been reopened by Einstein,[1] who has discovered some missing pages of the Vienna additions to the opera. His discovery seems to show that the hitherto accepted version is incomplete and inaccurate. After Leporello's escape from Zerlina, in the new version, Masetto returns with Elvira and Zerlina. They find that Leporello has gone. Zerlina asks Masetto where he has been, and he tells them that it was Heaven's will that he should save a lady in distress. After he left them previously he had not gone far before he heard cries. "I saw a woman weeping and a man fleeing," he says, "I tried to follow him, but he escaped out of sight. From what the girl told me of his appearance, and his manner, I believe that it was Don Giovanni."[2] Zerlina determines to tell Ottavio of this new misdemeanour, and she and Masetto go off, leaving Elvira alone on the stage. This new tale of woe naturally excites Elvira to pour out her sorrows and give vent to her feelings, and provides a dramatic reason for her recitative and aria.

It is suggested that this new discovery could advanta-geously be used in the theatre in the following way. As soon as Ottavio has concluded the recitative which precedes "Il mio tesoro," Elvira, Zerlina and Masetto should leave the stage and go into Anna's house. This gives effect to the words which he addresses to them in the recitative. "My

[1] See "Concerning some Recitatives in Don Giovanni," Music and Letters, October 1938.
[2] Masetto's story appears in the libretto of the Vienna version of the opera, but no music for it has hitherto been known. This missing music has been found by Einstein in the library of the Istituto musicale in Florence, and is set out in full in his article. Einstein explains that the current version of the recitative between Zerlina and Elvira is, in his opinion, a forgery.

Dino Borgioli as DON OTTAVIO in *Don Giovanni*
(Glyndebourne)

friends . . . remain in this house for a few hours." Then
Ottavio, left alone, sings his aria to Dent's zephyrs and
roses, and the impossibility of keeping Elvira, Zerlina and
Masetto occupied on the stage during his aria is obviated.
At the end of Ottavio's aria the curtain is drawn.

Then follows a short scene, which may conveniently be
staged in front of the curtain. Elvira and Zerlina walk in
on one side of the stage, and Masetto meets them coming
from the other. Zerlina begins this new scene with the
words *Ah, Masetto, Masetto, dove fosti finor?* ("Ah,
Masetto, Masetto, where have you been until now?")
Then follows Masetto's narrative with the music from the
Florence manuscript. At the end of it he goes off with
Zerlina to see Ottavio. Elvira's recitative "In quali
eccessi" and aria "Mi tradì quell' alma ingrata" follow
absolutely logically upon this. Masetto's new recitative
gives point to Elvira's music, which is thus retained, and
the whole scene between Zerlina and Leporello is left out
as before.

Scene 3

The first matter of importance in this scene is that the
time, according to Don Giovanni's remark, is two o'clock
in the morning.[1] The only light is the moon. Don Giovanni says that it is almost lighter than by day, but it is
none the less night, and Leporello has difficulty in reading
the inscription on the Statue. At first Don Giovanni and
Leporello are laughing together, but they are presently
severely rebuked. The Statue of the murdered Commendatore is the first person of authority who calls Don
Giovanni to account for his misdeeds. His utterances are
terrible, and should send a cold shiver through the most

[1] See page 79 for a discussion on this point.

hard-bitten profligate. Mozart brings out their significance with masterly effect in the music. The whole scene, before the Statue speaks, is conducted in recitative. Then suddenly the Statue speaks in long weighty notes to the accompaniment of trombones. The last trump has almost sounded. In their context, these trombones carry enormous weight, for they have not been used previously in the opera. No effort should be spared to make these utterances of the Statue effective. The effect upon Leporello is overwhelming, as it should be upon the audience too.

It has come to be accepted that the Statue of the Commendatore should be an equestrian statue. Although the directions indicate that there should be several equestrian statues, they do not specifically direct that the Commendatore himself should be mounted. There is no reference to a horse in the text, and the producer may, therefore, consider the question upon its merits.

A mounted statue is undoubtedly dignified and impressive. Coming from a height, his words carry greater weight. Beside the tall figure on a horse, Don Giovanni and Leporello look very small, and the representative of the powers of Good towers suitably above their evil heads. However, surprise is the essence of this scene, and if the Commendatore is on a horse, there must be other equestrian statues which would tax the resources of all but the largest theatres. Were his the only one, his identity would never for a moment be in doubt.

There is a lot to be said for dispensing with the horse. A pedestal to the statue will serve to give him dignity, and if there are several similar statues his identity will not at once be revealed. Observe that it is not until Leporello has read the inscription on the statue that he and Don Giovanni realize that it is the Commendatore who has spoken. If this scene and the Commendatore's appearance in the supper room are considered together, as they must be, the absurdity of an equestrian statue is at once apparent. It is unlikely that the stone Commendatore can detach himself from his stone horse, and so he must appear in the last scene mounted on his horse. This has been done, e.g. at Salzburg in 1934, but the appearance of a horse in the supper room is bound to look ridiculous, and detract from the indescribable horror that should be created by the entrance of the strange visitor. Also Leporello indicates that he hears the steps (presumably footsteps) of the stone guest as he approaches.

Scene 4

Back in Anna's house, for the last song. The only direction is "Dark room," but the house is better than a chapel, as has been suggested by some writers. The scene reveals little new in the characters of Anna and Ottavio. Only Ottavio emerges as a slightly less insipid figure than before. Here he at any rate has the courage to call his beloved Anna cruel, an epithet which it takes her a whole aria to refute! On the other hand the scene serves as an essential interlude in the drama. In the cemetery, and in the supper room, the music reaches the heights of dramatic intensity, and the effect of the supper scene and of Don Giovanni's descent into Hell is enhanced by Anna's lyrical music which separates it from the drama of the cemetery.

Scene 5

The first thorny problem here is whether or not to introduce some women to keep Don Giovanni company at supper. There is no reference to them in the text, and they have no music to sing. Don Giovanni and Leporello have nothing to say to them, which makes their presence seem superfluous. Further, Don Giovanni is a hunter, not a collector. His pleasure in female company is entirely the pleasure of conquest. It is true that Don Giovanni sings "Vivan le femmine!", which at first sight seems to refer to women who are there with him. In fact, these words are only part of a general toast, *Vivan le femmine, viva il buon vino!* ("Here's to women and wine"), which Don Giovanni mockingly gives to Elvira, in response to her appeal to him to lead a new life. These words, therefore, are no justification for the presence of the women. Mozart himself, in a fragment of a translation of the opera which has survived, speaks of women at Don Giovanni's supper table.[1] If there is no other good reason for introducing the women, it is submitted that this, by itself, is not enough, and even this fragment of a translation is said by some to be spurious.

There is a band of musicians in the room, who are to entertain the master of the house during supper. This would be the normal procedure in the household of a gentleman of standing. The band is playing a popular selection. Their first piece is from Martin's opera *Una cosa rara,* their second from Sarti's *I due litiganti,* and their third, Mozart's own "Non più andrai," from *Le Nozze di Figaro.* The first two operas are long since forgotten, but for Mozart's audience in Prague the pieces taken from them were popular favourites, as also was the song from Mozart's own opera. Leporello refers to each piece in turn as it is played. *Bravi! Cosa rara,* greets the first; *Evvivano i litiganti* the second; *Questa poi la conosco pur troppo*

---

[1] Jahn, vol. II, p. 544. *See also* an article by Richard Capell in *The Daily Telegraph,* dated May 6th, 1936.

("You know this one only too well") the third. It has been suggested that the first and third of these remarks refer to the particular dish which Leporello is at that moment handing to his master, and that the second does not appear in some versions of the text. This explanation does not really help even if it is valid, for it assumes that Mozart introduced this music pointlessly. Why should Leporello say *Bravi* (plural) if he is not referring to the musicians? And it does not require much imagination to assume that *questa* applies to *musica*. Clearly Mozart intended to introduce these popular pieces, as being the normal sort of music which a household band would be expected to play during supper.[1]

Don Giovanni and Leporello are by now in a merry mood. They have entirely forgotten the Statue and can well afford to mock Elvira, whose last pathetic attempt to persuade Don Giovanni to reform and return to her is not only an essential dramatic preparation for the terrors that are to come, but incidentally follows logically upon the words of her aria "Mi tradì."

The scene darkens, and the imposing figure of the Statue bursts in. Leporello crouches under the table, leaving his master to deal with his unwelcome guest. The latter dominates the scene, and there must be no shirking of the full dramatic and terrifying effect of his appearance. When the end comes, he should take the opportunity of disappearing behind the screen of the flames and earthquakes that occur at this moment, for his supernatural visit is spoiled if he turns round and walks out! (He does not wait to see Don Giovanni's end, probably because in the first performance Giuseppe Lolli had to hurry off to change into Masetto's clothes.) Don Giovanni's descent into hell

---

[1] It is instructive to study Dent's English version of this episode.

is best achieved by lighting effects, and there is no need for the whole scene to collapse.

There can be a pause after this, during which the normal lighting of the stage is resumed. The other characters enter, accompanied (according to the directions) by Ministers of Justice. It may be supposed that these have been summoned by Ottavio, but they are not wanted after all, because Heaven has intervened instead. They are better left out. Leporello now tells the grim story of Don Giovanni's end, and the way is clear for a discussion of petty personal affairs. Anna staves off Ottavio for another year, and even at the end of that period she probably will put him off again. Poor Ottavio! Throughout the opera he has played a very negative part. At first he was justifiably reluctant to take vengeance on Don Giovanni until satisfied of his guilt. But the events in the ballroom convinced him that Don Giovanni was the murderer of Anna's father, and he has let the whole of the second Act drift by without taking any steps! His relief when Heaven intervenes and takes revenge for him is obvious, and he is now only too anxious to persuade Anna to forget the whole thing and marry him. At the end he is back again at the same point where he was on his first appearance, entreating Anna to look to him for father and bridegroom. Ottavio must remain an ineffective figure, but it is submitted that there is nothing in his conduct or in his music which is substantially inconsistent with Hoffmann's interpretation of his character. Ottavio should be presented as a "dandy," and he should have a large fancy lace handkerchief hanging from his sleeve!

Anna reveals a certain amount of feeling for Ottavio, particularly at the end of the opera in "Non mi dir"; but even if Hoffmann was wrong—and he may have been—in

inferring that Don Giovanni seduced her, he was not so far
out in estimating her opinion of Ottavio. She uses him as
a chaperon, and his moral support is invaluable to her, but
she consistently repulses his practical advances and will
have nothing of sympathy or affection from him.

Elvira decides to seek consolation in the veil. She was,
or at any rate considered herself to be, Don Giovanni's
wife. Right to the last she loved him and would have
taken him back, and now that he is gone there is nothing
left for her. Zerlina and Masetto resume their interrupted
honeymoon. Don Giovanni's intervention in their mutual
happiness was but a passing cloud, and both are ready to
forget and forgive. Leporello is to find a new and, he
hopes, less exacting master.

The business of the opera is concluded. The curtain
falls, and the final sextet can be sung in front of it. While
it is sung the lights of the auditorium may be turned up,
for singers and audience join together in pointing the
moral. Society has won its victory, and the profligate who
sought to question its standards has suffered a suitable
fate!

III

COSÌ FAN TUTTE

COSÌ FAN TUTTE
(All women are the same)

or "La scuola degli amanti"
(The School for Lovers)

Opera buffa in Two Acts, by Lorenzo Da Ponte

Fiordiligi ⎫ ladies of Ferrara, sisters living in	⎧ Soprano
Dorabella ⎭ Naples	⎩ Soprano
Guglielmo ⎫ their lovers	⎧ Bass
Ferrando ⎭	⎩ Tenor
Despina, a maid	Soprano
Don Alfonso, a philosophic old man . .	Baritone

The scene is laid in Naples.

The opera was first produced in Vienna on January 26th, 1790.

SYNOPSIS OF THE STORY
ACT I
Scene 1. *A Tavern*

Two officers, Guglielmo and Ferrando, sing the praises of their sweethearts, Fiordiligi and Dorabella. Their older friend, Don Alfonso, laughs at them, and dares to pour cold water on their hot-headed enthusiasm, and to ask whether the ladies are goddesses or merely ordinary human beings. The officers insist upon a duel with anyone who questions their lovers' integrity, but Don Alfonso laughs again, and suggests that the ladies' affections be put to the test. The officers agree, and wager a hundred guineas on their lovers' constancy, and promise loyally to obey Don Alfonso's orders in carrying out the wager.

Scene 2. *The Garden of the Ladies' House*

Fiordiligi and Dorabella enlarge upon the merits of their officers, but they are interrupted by Don Alfonso, who comes to tell them that their lovers have been called away to the war—the first step in the wager! The officers come to bid farewell, and to the sound of the drums they are taken off in a boat to the war. When they are gone, Don Alfonso and the ladies join in a solemn trio wishing them God-speed upon their voyage.

Scene 3. *A Room in the Ladies' House*

Despina, the maid, prepares her mistresses' chocolate, and is surprised to find them depressed. On learning the reason for their grief, she laughs at them for taking life so seriously, and horrifies them by suggesting that their lovers' absence is a good opportunity for amusement. The ladies leave the room in anger, and Don Alfonso calls to let Despina into the secret of the wager. He introduces to her the officers dressed as Albanian merchants, who have come to win the affections of her mistresses. Ferrando will take Fiordiligi, and Guglielmo, Dorabella. Don Alfonso leaves the house, and the ladies come in, appalled to hear strange men talking to Despina. In spite of the ardent advances of the "merchants," and in spite of Don Alfonso's reappearance and recognition of them as his oldest friends, the ladies will have none of it, and are horror-struck at this intrusion upon their grief. Don Alfonso has lost the first round!

Scene 4. *The Garden*

In furtherance of the plot, the "Albanians" disturb the ladies, who are talking together in the garden, by rushing in apparently dying from poison. They have attempted suicide in view of the rejection of their suit! Don Alfonso and Despina exhort the ladies to console their visitors, and comfort them in their distress. Despina disappears, and comes in again dressed up as a doctor, whose magnetic cure restores the men to life. Their affectionate advances again terrify the ladies, who are assured by the "doctor" that this is the natural result of the treatment. By this means the ladies' resistance is temporarily broken down, but still Don Alfonso shows no sign of winning his wager.

ACT II

Scene 1. *The House*

After the events of the previous scene, the ladies are more ready to listen to Despina's worldly counsel, and decide to accept the approaches of the "Albanians." They are warned by Don Alfonso to prepare for a serenade.

Scene 2. *The Garden*

The "Albanians," prompted by Don Alfonso, serenade the ladies, who are led on by Despina. At the end the two pairs of lovers are left alone. Guglielmo is amazed and horrified for Ferrando's sake to find that Dorabella takes his advances seriously. Ferrando has no such success, and Fiordiligi at once wildly regrets her momentary infidelity. When the two men meet again, Guglielmo has to show Ferrando his own portrait which Dorabella has given to him as a keepsake. Poor Ferrando!

Scene 3. *The House*

Fiordiligi, afraid of being tempted again, calls for Guglielmo's uniform, for she intends to join her lover at the war. Dorabella and Despina laugh at her constancy, and leave her alone. She is surprised by Ferrando, and after a desperate mental struggle, agrees to accept him. The officers have lost their wager!

Scene 4. *The Garden*

The wedding breakfast is ready, and the ladies are married to their "Albanian" admirers by Despina, disguised as a notary. As soon as the contract is signed, the sound of drums heralds the officers' return. The "Albanians" are pushed into an inner room, and reappear again in their proper clothes. In the haste of the moment the marriage contract was left on the floor, and is discovered by Guglielmo. The knot is now untied, all is explained and forgiven, and the ladies once more return to their original lovers.

THE OPERA

THE third and last opera written by Mozart and Da Ponte remains the least known of the three. It has been called the musician's opera, thereby implying that it is a work that can have no general appeal. This is true in the sense that it has no "catchy" tunes, and that its music is less immediately approachable than that of the others. Further, it has never acquired a permanent English translation, though this in itself should be no bar to popularity. All the same, as long as the title remains incomprehensible, the opera tends to be inaccessible. It might well be called "All women are the same," or better still "The School for Lovers," which is its subtitle. The real cause, however, of the opera's failure to win universal approval has been its story.

Right from the beginning of its history the conventional approach to the opera has been to condemn the libretto and praise the music. It was considered shocking that such beautiful music should be squandered on a wanton story of immorality. Numerous attempts have therefore been made to free the music from its "unworthy" surroundings, and to provide it with a story to which no objection could be taken. For a full account of the various versions of the opera which have been prepared with this object in view, the reader is referred to Jahn. None of these versions has survived, or could survive, because Da Ponte's libretto is so perfectly matched by Mozart's music that the two are inseparable. If those who objected to the story had studied Da Ponte's libretto in its original language, they would have seen that his handling of the subject is utterly unexceptionable.[1] There is no bald immorality, but instead a wonderfully delicate unreality. The opera does not set out to deal with an actual world; its characters are too superficial to be called human. In writing about the story, the word "love" must be used, but love in a real sense has no meaning for such people as these. What is their love in comparison with that of the great lovers of Shakespeare's plays? How can Ferrando and Dorabella be set beside Romeo and Juliet? The two pairs of names have only to be written together to show how shallow is the so-called "love" that is the subject-matter of *Così fan Tutte*. Here is no story of the tragedy of crossed lovers, nothing to excite the heart to pity, nothing to stir the emotions.

Taken at its face value, the story of the opera sounds impossible, and no translation can perfectly reproduce the delicacy and wit of Da Ponte's libretto. Its style is of a type that can only be expressed in the Italian language, and cannot but lose everything of its refinement, everything of its atmosphere by translation.

The charm of *Così fan Tutte* lies in the perfect union of music and libretto. Both find the precise medium for dealing with this artificial subject. Both are delicate, refined and stilted. Both achieve the most extraordinary subtlety of expression, and both are pompous and cynical by turns. Take Fiordiligi's great aria "Come scoglio." What right has she thus to adopt the grand manner? What emotion has stirred within her to justify the style and mode of expression associated with heroines? In the music and words of this aria, Mozart and Da Ponte have adopted and yet gently satirized the grand operatic aria, using the metaphor technique with all its force.

[1] [Christopher Benn spoke Italian and German, having studied language and music in both countries.]

Even to-day the subject is often condemned. On the one hand, in Germany for instance, the opera is taken heavily, and on the other hand, the average Englishman is inclined to think of it as a pure farce. It is a mistake to regard *Così fan Tutte* too seriously. Da Ponte is not Ibsen, seeking to unmask the conventions of society. His story is pure fantasy, not a social study of a real world. Society must indeed be insecure if it needs to fear the harmless satire of the libretto of *Così fan Tutte*. The music shows that neither a too serious nor yet a farcical approach to the opera is right, for on the one hand much of it is serious and sad, and on the other hand much of it is light-hearted. The story is straightforward and absolutely logical, and in each moment of the opera the music shows whether it is serious or light-hearted. The most difficult task which faces the producer of this opera is the differentiation between the tragic and comic. Too often the tragic side of the opera has been altogether ignored. Perhaps "tragic" is scarcely the word, although Mozart has so infused these superficial characters with emotion, that it is at times easy to forget that their feelings are not very deep. There is no real tragedy for people like these, but such is the subtlety of the style of the opera, that it nearly approaches to the medium generally associated with deeper emotions.

As will be noticed in considering the opera scene by scene, the serious moments are numerous and cannot be ignored. Too often at performances of *Così fan Tutte*, there is a terrible conflict between ear and eye. The ear hears the most serious and deeply moving music, while the eye sees a slapstick farce proceeding on the stage. For a true appreciation of the greatness of the music of *Così fan Tutte*, it is essential that the balance between the tragic and the comic elements of the opera be nicely held.

Costume design for FIORDILIGI—*Così fan Tutte*
(Sadlers Wells)

The true view of *Così fan Tutte* must surely be that it
is an artificial work, not a farce. In a sense it is a parody
of grand opera. On the face of it, it deals with the greatest
force in human life, namely love, and portrays the reactions
of four people in the face of the stress and strain of the
emotions that accompany falling in and out of love. It is
a parody, because those emotions have no real foundations
in this story and the characters have no justification for
expressing them. Deeper love than theirs, and more real
anguish, would be necessary to account for such violent,
and apparently sincere, protestations and sighings! The
authors are poking fun at the lovers. They make them
speak the language of real tragedy, and behave as though
actuated by great depth of feeling.

At first sight, there is good reason to suppose that the
opera should be presented as a pure farce. The wager
itself, which is the basis of the story, is apparently nothing
but a piece of absurd fooling. And what are the dressing
up of the officers in Oriental garb, and the miraculous
magnetic cure, if not the ordinary properties of a farce?
All these things, however, are capable of reasonable explanation, and are not intended to colour the whole opera.
They are all consistent with the view that the opera is an
artificial parody.

The whole meaning of the story must depend upon the
wager, and, as will be observed, it is essential that the first
scene should be as realistic as possible. By contrast, the
rest of the opera then appears as a dream. The Eastern
garb of the officers, and also the magnet, both have a
reasonable explanation, as will be seen when the individual
episodes of the opera come to be discussed. On the other
side, the whole point of the music is destroyed if the
farcical view of the opera is upheld. How can such heart-

rending strains as accompany so much of it be reconciled with farce? Obviously, such music must be taken seriously, and given its due weight. Although this serious element of the music may be cynical, it must be played and sung with due regard for its face value, or its point is lost. The cynicism needs no underlining.

Is the opera, perhaps, something of a thrust at the superficiality of the structure of society? Seen from this angle, is not its cynicism just as full of point to-day as it was when it was first written? How empty are the lives of the four lovers, how devoid of any real purpose! Do not the illustrated papers of to-day betray the same emptiness and frivolity in the lives of men and women? Are not the gossip columns recording in all seriousness the petty activities of society just as much of a comment on the uselessness of life as the words and music of *Così fan Tutte?* This is not to say that the opera is a serious social study, but merely a reason for its acceptability to-day. After all, there is great similarity between the satire of *Così fan Tutte* and the modern revue. Both are mirrors of life, adopting the phraseology and habits of a real world in order to show how unreal it is. *Così fan Tutte,* then, must be presented with an air of seriousness, and its power to entertain must depend upon the subtlety of the producer in letting it speak for itself, and not on any exaggeration of its humour.

THE CHARACTERS

An examination of the characters will make this clear at once. Don Alfonso and Despina are straightforward. They are real people, and they only appear to be cynical because they are seen against an artificial background.

Their counsel is worldly, but none the less human, and the success of their schemings depends upon the age-old truth that everyone must learn for himself.

At the beginning of the opera the men will not listen to Don Alfonso nor the ladies to Despina, and it is only in the hard school of practical experience that their views are upheld. They only venture to point out that human nature has its weaknesses, advice that cannot, of course, appeal to headstrong youth!

The officers are seen at the beginning of the opera as ardent lovers. Naturally Don Alfonso's observations fall on deaf ears, for they are living in the clouds. In the throes of blind adoration—it is not to be described as love —they pay no heed to his devil's advocacy. In the first scene, their youth and inexperience are perfectly portrayed. Their music is heroic and full of purpose, but their feelings are seen to be empty enough against the saner background of Don Alfonso's experience. There is nothing to underline here. As the opera proceeds they awaken, all too slowly at first, to the realities of the situation. At the end, they have ceased to be mere boys, full of the overbearing pride of youth, and have grown into saner and more experienced men. All the different shades of their feelings in their progress between these two extremes are drawn with the reality of a drama in the grand manner. Their very seriousness in the face of what are, after all, trivial experiences shows their artificiality. Who would really be so moved by "love" such as this? They are the essence of an elegant society, caring all for pleasure, having no conception of their own emptiness. Their schooling is a bitter one; as will be seen at the turning-point of the opera, when the joke begins to have alarming consequences, they are overcome with grief—but only momentarily. As soon as they have both suffered the unfortunate experience of having their eyes opened to the infidelity of their lovers, they are at once ready to accept such conduct as normal. How quickly the pangs of remorse disappear! Clearly this was no very deep-rooted love, which can thus lightly be forgotten. The supreme subtlety of the drawing of the characters of these officers is seen when it is realized that on their own personalities are superimposed the personalities of the Albanian merchants! After the first scene, the officers are living one part and playing another!

The ladies, too, endure a bitter schooling in the opera. They start as a pair of flippant and irresponsible girls, wrapped up in themselves, engrossed in a blissful love-affair. Nothing can disturb their rosy horizon or upset their peace of mind. Then all of a sudden comes the bitter blow of their lovers' departure for the war. That alone, for the moment, is sufficient to shatter their dream and to reduce them to utter misery. Worse experiences are in store for them, and in the course of their wooing by the "Albanians" they learn of mental strife and anguish of a kind unknown to them before. For Fiordiligi the struggle is terrific; after her first agreement to accept the suit of her "Albanian" admirer, she wildly regrets her decision. The realization that her fidelity could so easily be shaken is terrifying to her. Dorabella is more light-hearted, and her forwardness is set off against Fiordiligi's greater depth of character.

Where is the justification in this story for the high-sounding words and ardent feelings which these ladies express? How petty and how thoroughly cheap they are. Guglielmo is right when in the heat of the moment he speaks of Dorabella as a woman who is not worth two sous. What a travesty to talk of this as love; here is nothing but a story of stupid infidelity.

All this might be taken to imply that the opera is a sordid story of immorality, and so it sounds. But its artificiality saves it from any such charge. It is so delicately contrived and so artificial that there is absolutely nothing that can be regarded as immoral.

Così fan Tutte is essentially a miniature; it is beautifully rounded off, and worked out from scene to scene in extraordinary detail. Of the three librettos which Da Ponte wrote for Mozart, *Così fan Tutte* is his only original work. As we have seen, *Figaro* was freely taken from Beaumarchais' play, and *Don Giovanni* from Bertati's version of the story. Even *Così fan Tutte* is popularly supposed to be based on true occurrences, and to have been suggested to the authors as a suitable subject for an opera by the Emperor. Further, Da Ponte's handling of the subject follows well-established lines. As Jahn points out,[1] it is little more than a hotch-pot of all the elements which went to make up the conventional *opera buffa*. When all is said, however, Da Ponte's libretto emerges triumphant. His conception is unpretentious and essentially artificial, but his pattern is perfectly symmetrical. There are six characters, three men and three women, and every possible combination of these is exploited to the full. Each character is seen, not so much by himself, as in relation to all the others. This pattern is merely the foundation upon which Da Ponte builds an incredible series of situations, providing an opportunity for the expression of the whole gamut of human emotion.

[1] Vol. II, page 645.

THE PRODUCTION

Così fan Tutte does not present such difficult problems of production as *Don Giovanni* or *Die Zauberflöte*. In the Glyndebourne setting of *Così fan Tutte*, the stage is divided off into an inner and an outer scene. The outer scene, with the curtain drawn across the inner scene, represents a spacious passage. When the inner scene is a room, the passage serves as an extension of it; when a garden, as a natural approach to it from the house. The passage remains constant throughout the opera, and the inner scene can therefore be changed while the action proceeds in the passage. It also provides a perfect setting for Don Alfonso's addresses to the audience and for the soliloquies. Further, this double scene has the effect. of putting the whole opera in a frame, thus creating a certain impression of artificiality.

Così fan Tutte is a very long opera, and consequently it has become the practice to shorten it for performance. This practice is adopted at Glyndebourne, and it therefore seems of interest to note the numbers which are omitted in the Glyndebourne production. They are as follows:

Act I, Scene 2. Recitative and Duet for Guglielmo and Ferrando, pages 49 to 52.[1]

Act II, Scene 2. Aria for Ferrando, pages 239 to 246.

Scene 2. Recitative and Cavatina for Ferrando, pages 270 to 274.

Scene 3. Aria for Dorabella, pages 282 to 287.

Scene 3. Part of Duet for Fiordiligi and Ferrando, pages 294 to 295.

Scene 4. Part of Chorus and Quartet of Lovers, pages 312 to 318.

[1] The page numbers refer to the vocal score published by Breitkopf and Härtel, Leipzig.

In addition to these principal cuts, there are omissions from the recitatives of the opera, which are too numerous to be set out here. By means of alterations in the music and in the words of the recitatives, an attempt has been made to achieve these cuts without disturbing the story or the meaning of the scenes. In one instance, however, the effect is disastrous. Nevertheless (although this is perhaps more a matter for current criticism than for a permanent record such as this book), it is a thousand pities that the opera cannot be performed complete. As it was conceived and written by its authors the opera is quite perfect from the point of view of form. Unlike *Don Giovanni,* it was all written at one time, and was not revised or added to later. There is no question of musical merit involved, and the choice of which pieces shall be left out and which retained is purely arbitrary. In ordinary circumstances, at an evening performance after a long day's work, a shortening of the second Act is justifiable. Glyndebourne, on the other hand, is a festival opera house, to attend which the audience must devote most of an afternoon and evening. It cannot be too strongly urged, therefore, that *Così fan Tutte* should be performed there in its entirety.

ACT I

Scene 1

On the face of it, the events of this opening scene, upon which the intrigue of the whole opera is based, are fantastically absurd. Whoever heard of such a wager as this, or of two officers with so little sense of humour that they take the chaff of an old man so seriously as to draw swords? Yet something convincing must be made of this scene, or the whole of the rest of the opera falls to the ground. Honour being a matter of importance to a soldier, it is not perhaps unreasonable that the lovers should be prepared to carry out the terms of their wager once it is made. The problem is, how to make the wager itself appear in the least convincing.

Often the scene is set in a bright-looking room, or in a garden for all the world reminiscent of a Continental café at tea-time (as at Salzburg in 1934). The officers are spick-and-span, smoking a churchwarden with Don Alfonso over a quiet cup of tea! They sing the praises of their ladies in the best operatic manner, without any particular enthusiasm, and it appears improbable, to say the least, that they would ever risk a penny for the sake of their convictions. Nothing is more surprising than that Don Alfonso should succeed in persuading them to put their feelings to the test.

Such a presentation renders the scene dull, whereas in fact it is the most dramatic and theatrically effective in the opera. At Glyndebourne there is no compromising of the drama. The scene is set in a dingy little room in a "pub." It is dark, the tap-room boy is asleep on the floor, and the candles, stuck in bottles on the table, are nearly spent. The officers and their friend have clearly made a night of it, and the grim light of approaching dawn has not yet arrived to restore them to their senses. Merriment and drink have done their worst, and at this stage of the evening they are capable of anything. What more natural than that they should wildly and recklessly sing their lovers' praises, and be prepared to do battle with anyone who dares to gainsay them? The music is hilarious and full of life: played without restraint, it builds up a climax that will bring down the house.

Thus the reality of this scene is clearly brought out;

Costume design for GUGLIELMO and FERRANDO—*Così fan Tutte*
(Sadlers Wells)

almost exaggerated. The whole secret of the Glyndebourne production of *Così fan Tutte* is the suggestion of
actuality and drama in this first scene, after which the rest
seems like a dream. So the opera is made to live. Here
in the atmosphere of drink and merry-making, the wager
is a reality, and the story has a thoroughly convincing
send-off. The whole of the remainder of the opera is
artificial, a fantasy compared with the first scene. Once
the wager has been made at the height of a drunken evening, the parties to it carry it out without question, never
looking back to see the futility of the occasion on which
it was made!

Scene 2

In the garden of their villa the two sisters vie with each
other in extolling the merits of their lovers. They appear
to be in an utterly frittering and irresponsible mood. What
are the merits of their sweethearts that so attract them?
Intellect, character. Not so!

"Where would you find a more noble aspect or such a
fine mouth?" asks Fiordiligi, almost as if she were speaking of a new horse! On the face of the music appears joy-
ful rapture; innocent abandonment to superficial thoughts
of love. For the audience there is subtlety in this. They
know what disillusionment and change of heart are in store
for the ladies, and this delicious music is full of satirical
meaning. Of course Mozart and Da Ponte have piled on
the humour here. The ladies protest of the lasting quality
of their love a good deal more than is necessary. They
exaggerate the unique qualities of their officers.

All the same this scene is a mirror of life. It is by no
means an unreal picture of the mentality of many women,
who flit through the world without thought or care. The

whole atmosphere of the music so far is gloriously artificial. Don Alfonso's entrance, with the dreadful news of the soldiers' imminent departure, drops like a bomb upon the ladies' fantasy. This is the occasion for pure comedy, and his stammering reluctance to tell the ladies the news is perfectly matched by his limping music. Then at once the officers appear, and real sadness pervades the music almost until the end of the scene.

It is at this point that the first substantial cut is made in the Glyndebourne production of the opera. Here is left out a section of recitative and a duet for Guglielmo and Ferrando. It cannot be said that this omission upsets the meaning of the story, and it does not disturb the atmosphere of the music. A large painting would not be cut down to economize on the frame, but much must be endured to save time in the opera house!

This is a part that is often mishandled. The officers' leave-taking and departure are treated as the moment for unrestrained fooling. The ladies are made to weep crocodile tears, and generally to give the impression that they know of the joke of which they are the victims. Yet this music without any exception is serious and sad. The sisters are absolutely overcome, and the officers desperate at the plight to which they have driven their lovers. At the end, just before their departure, they turn back for a final embrace. It seems to be a general practice to raise a laugh at this point by making the officers embrace the wrong girls, and then hastily, amid blushes, rectify the mistake. This manœuvre is invariably a huge success, and may seem very funny, but it reveals a complete misunderstanding of the music, and effectively shatters the whole atmosphere of sorrow that it has created. Here is a moment of real despair. The ladies are losing their lovers, and the officers, if not really going off to the war, are embarking on the test of their ladies' fidelity—for them perhaps a far more hazardous adventure even than battle! This part of the scene is genuinely sad, and the farce can be reserved for the other occasions, when the music itself pokes fun at the characters.

Again, where is there more poignant music to be found than in the trio after the officers' departure? Even Don Alfonso has for the moment forgotten his cynicism and joins whole-heartedly with the ladies in bidding his friends God-speed upon their voyage. At the end of the trio, after the officers' departure, the inner curtain is drawn, leaving Don Alfonso to address his cynical remarks about women to the ladies in the audience!

It is wrong for Don Alfonso to be portrayed as a hard character. There is surely no bitterness, no sting in his cynicism. He is rather the mellow old man who enjoys a joke at the expense of the young and innocent! Nor is there anything coarse in his character. His manners to-wards Despina, for instance, are a model of courtesy, and there is no suggestion of stupid flirting, or of "pairing him off" with her. He is essentially a gentleman whose ripe old age has not deprived him of a sense of humour.

Scene 3

This scene introduces Despina, the most entrancing character in the opera, and with her appearance the atmosphere changes from sadness to glorious hilarity. It is obvious from the first moment of her entry that, although unknown to them, she rules the roost in her mistresses' establishment!

The audience rightly laughs with her at the ladies' misery, for this episode is one of unbroken light-heartedness. Their prostration is heavily exaggerated by Mozart and Da Ponte to make their later fickleness all the clearer. How artificial! Here in the music is all the atmosphere of dreadful tragedy and grief, accompanying nothing but the empty tears of two stupid girls.

Then Don Alfonso appears, and as might be expected, he readily persuades Despina to fall in with his plan, and introduces her to the officers in disguise. The grotesque costumes in which they appear is the chief reason, perhaps, for the opera being considered as a mere farce. How is it possible for the sisters to take two such fantastic creatures in the least seriously, and how is it that they do not at once see through the joke that is being played upon them? Even this seemingly absurd element in the story has its probability in actual fact. Dent[1] says that Da Ponte originally planned that the scene of the opera should not be Naples, but Trieste, where the presence of merchants from Albania was no unusual spectacle. Thus there is nothing in the arrival of these gentlemen to arouse the suspicions of the ladies, and it is by no means unlikely that they should have made the acquaintance of Don Alfonso on one of their business visits to the city.

In the midst of the fun of this scene there is no forecast of the shadows that darken the second Act. As yet there is no mental struggle for the ladies, and nothing but hilarity for the officers, who still regard the whole thing as a joke. Note that Dorabella already shows her colours as the more dashing of the two sisters. After the strangers have been formally introduced by Don Alfonso—and their visit thus regularized to a certain extent!—Dorabella's first reaction to their passionate advances is not horror at all. *Sorella! che faciamo?* ("Sister, what shall we do?") is her

[1] Page 295.

only comment! This hesitation is contrasted with Fiordiligi's expression of steadfastness. Her love will stand
firm like a rock amid storm and tempest. This great aria
is sheer nonsense when analysed in its context, but as a
piece of masterly satire it is unmatched anywhere else in
the opera.

In the Glyndebourne production the inner curtain is
drawn for Ferrando's aria, and this and the rest of the scene
are sung in the passage.

Scene 4

The ladies are the centre of this glorious finale. From
their resolute beginning, and firm refusal to entertain the
suits of their new admirers, they slowly begin to change.
The desperate attempt at suicide by the men is too much
for them, and reluctantly, but only as it were for medical
reasons, and against their better judgment, they show
signs of weakening. The whole of this scene is light-
hearted, and all the other characters are playing up to the
ladies with the utmost amusement. Even the men enjoy
the joke, for as yet their advances have not been seriously
received and they are still confident of their lovers' fidelity.

Despina's appearance as a doctor, and the miraculous
magnetic cure which she effects on the officers, seems at
first sight to be yet another reason for regarding the opera
as a farce. The great Mesmer was then at the height of his
fame, and Despina's fantastic magnet[1] was introduced as
a sly cut at the great doctor, just as topical jokes at the
expense of the famous are introduced into a modern revue.
This incident must be considered by itself and not as
colouring the whole of the rest of the opera. Mesmer was

[1] Not, please, a nutmeg grater, as used in the production in Regent's
Park in 1938!

an old and valued friend of Mozart and his family, for as early as 1768 *Bastien et Bastienne* had been performed in the garden of his house in the Landsstrasse, where Mozart was always sure of a welcome.

Act II

Scene 1

The sisters, under the worldly guidance of Despina, are gradually coming round to the view that perhaps after all there is no particular harm in receiving the attentions of their new admirers. Even Dorabella is not a little uneasy about the dangers of the situation, but Despina is always ready with a worldly, if dishonest, answer! "Heaven will be watching us," says Dorabella. "But we are on the earth, not in Heaven." "What if we are discovered?" "Say that the strangers are coming to see me." Thus Despina dispels their doubts. In the end they go so far as to decide that Fiordiligi shall take the fair one, and Dorabella the dark. The music here returns to the light-hearted style of the first scene in the garden. Even Fiordiligi, who at first somewhat reluctantly falls in with the advice of her more dashing sister, has for the moment forgotten Guglielmo, and is quite ready to discuss which of the visitors shall be hers.

There is something irresistibly cynical about this scene, for it is a repetition of the mood of the earlier scene, when the girls were eagerly discussing the merits of their real lovers, and Mozart has gently hinted at the style of the earlier music.

At the end of the girls' duet they step in front of the inner curtain, which is drawn across, and before they go off, Don Alfonso warns them to prepare for the serenade.

This is an admirable example of the use of the double stage, for the officers now come on, nervously learning their words for the serenade, which they begin to sing in front of the curtain. This enables the inner scene to be changed without interruption, and when, at the commencement of—

Scene 2

the curtain is drawn in the middle of the serenade, it reveals the ladies waiting in the garden to receive it. Having paired off the lovers successfully, Don Alfonso and Despina step forward into the passage, apart from the main scene, to sing their little duet, "per carità partiamo." The scene now remains unchanged for some while.

The scene which follows is the central point of the opera. Until now the officers have taken the whole thing as a joke. They have willingly followed Don Alfonso's instructions and loyally played their part in the wager. So far it has been great fun, and they have been confident that they will win.

For the girls, too, there has as yet been nothing particularly serious. Once their initial reluctance to see or speak to anyone in their lovers' absence has been overcome, they have accepted Despina's worldly advice in a spirit of frivolity, never considering for a moment that there could be anything but innocent amusement in store for them. After this long period of light-heartedness, matters come to a head in this scene, when, for the first time, the "Albanians" are left alone with the sisters. Up to date they have only wooed them from a distance, but now that they are left alone, the realization suddenly comes to them that it is now too late to turn back, and that they must continue in earnest the suit which they have so frivolously begun. Ferrando recognizes this in his aside to Guglielmo *Eccoci alla gran crisi* ("Now we're at the turn-ing-point").

After the amusing opening remarks about the weather there is nothing whatever comic about this scene. Face to face with his brother officer's betrothed, the disguised Guglielmo is horrified to find that his suit is being taken seriously. At first, as he has done before, he upbraids her for joking and laughing at his advances, but this is only done to draw her out. What is his amazement when he discovers that, far from joking, she is completely serious. In this terrible moment Guglielmo's mind is in hopeless confusion. He finds himself first of all in the extraordinary position of making violent love to a strange woman. At first this was a joke, but now he realizes that he has awakened in her a passion for himself, dressed up as an Albanian merchant, a passion which he cannot reciprocate in the least. How terrifying to be in a position to exercise such power over a woman! Secondly, his integrity as an officer is at stake. He has betrayed the lover of a fellow officer, and he thinks ahead to the moment when he must render an account to Ferrando. Further, although he says nothing about it, his thoughts must be with his own Fior-diligi. He realizes that there was some foundation for Don Alfonso's cynicism about women, and if Dorabella has so easily been proved unfaithful, what of Fiordiligi?

Of her, however, he need not have been afraid. All along Fiordiligi has been more reluctant than her sister to forget her absent lover. She has never been very willing to receive her "Albanian" admirer. The serenade seemed a pleasant and innocent entertainment. Face to face with Ferrando, however, she realizes that the joke has gone too

Costume design for Masked Fantastic—*Così fan Tutte*
(Sadlers Wells)

far, and desperately regrets her momentary infidelity.

It is at this point that a cut is made with disastrous effect in the Glyndebourne production. Guglielmo and Dorabella have left the scene arm-in-arm, and Fiordiligi then runs on to the stage, with Ferrando after her. "You have taken away my peace of mind," she cries. "To make you happy," is his answer. "Cease molesting me." "I only ask for a look." "Go." Ferrando in desperation: "Do not hope for that until you turn your eyes less proudly towards me. Oh, Heaven! You look at me and then heave a sigh." Then comes Ferrando's aria, unfortunately cut at Glyndebourne. This begins in a spirit of optimism. "Ah, I see that you cannot resist my entreaty. . . . Your look, those dear sighs, are a ray of sweet light to my heart. Already you respond to my ardent desires." These words and the tender music to which they are sung evidently have no effect on Fiordiligi. Ferrando therefore changes the tune, and upbraids her for falsely raising his hopes. "Oh, cease, false hopes, her cruelty condemns me to die." At the end of the song he rushes off. This last method has had its effect, and Fiordiligi's first reaction is to run after him, and explain all.

"He's going; listen," she calls after him. But then on reflection, she changes her mind. "No; let him go, it is better that he should be out of my sight, rather than tempt me in my weakness. To what risks he exposes me. This is the well-deserved price to pay for my wrongdoing."

It is clear from this that at first Fiordiligi was resolved to flee from Ferrando, and dismiss him from her mind. His long aria has melted her, however, and now she recognizes the profound effect that he has worked in her life. Her feelings have gradually changed. At first she sought to gloss over any momentary thrill that she may have experienced. Now, after his long and passionate address, accompanied by such bewitching music, who could fail to be moved! Without the aria the carefully contrived effect is lost, and Fiordiligi's feelings change in a minute for no reason! She is still horrified at the thought of her weakness, but she has to acknowledge that Ferrando's ardent wooing has had a profound effect upon her. She may no longer ignore the feeling that he has aroused in her, and in her aria, "Per pietà," she implores her absent officer to forgive her. This aria is the most serious music in the opera.

When the officers meet to compare notes, Guglielmo has difficulty in restraining Ferrando's anger. He has to show him his own portrait given to him as a keepsake by Dorabella. What a dreadful moment for Ferrando, a doubly bitter blow, coming immediately after his over-confident assertion of his faith in the truth of his beloved! At this point, the inner curtain is drawn, leaving Guglielmo to sing his diatribe against women—a companion piece to Figaro's "Aprite un po"—to the audience. If, as is done at Glyndebourne, Ferrando's answering aria is to be left out, then Ferrando should leave the stage before Guglielmo's aria and return with Don Alfonso at the end of it. This is a cut that has no disturbing effect on the story, although here again there is no question of musical merit by which to decide which of the two arias, if either, is to be omitted. The two arias are perfectly balanced, one against the other —Guglielmo by now disillusioned and reckless, Ferrando still heartbroken at his betrayal.

Scene 3

Despina congratulates Dorabella on her conquest, but Fiordiligi is desperately unhappy. "I'm in love," she says, "but not only with Guglielmo!" She has to admit that Ferrando has worked a change in her. Here is seen the necessity for retaining Ferrando's aria in the previous scene. Without this there is nothing to explain Fiordiligi's mental struggle. In her heart of hearts she knows that she should be faithful to Guglielmo, but in spite of herself she cannot banish this feeling of love for the disguised Ferrando. Despina is now aided and abetted by Dorabella in her efforts to make Fiordiligi give in. Dorabella is by now absolutely oblivious of the consequences of her amorous adventure!

"What if our lovers return?" asks Fiordiligi. "So much the worse for them; by then we shall be married, and shall be thousands of miles away!" is all the response that she gets from her sister.

At this point there is an aria for Dorabella, in which she explains the fickleness of love. This might be Despina speaking, such is the change that has been wrought in Dorabella! This aria is left out in the Glyndebourne production. Here again the recitatives are arranged so that the cut does not disturb the sense. All the same, it is the cumulative effect of all Despina's worldly encouragement, and now this outlook of her sister, that drives Fiordiligi to call for her lover's uniform, and free herself from base temptation by following him to the field of battle. She knows that unless she tears herself from her surroundings and throws herself into some new enterprise, she will never wholly eradicate the effect that Ferrando has had upon her. At this point, although the spectacle of Fiordiligi dressing up may be funny enough, the music should be played with due seriousness. Mozart is laughing at, not with her, and the scene on the stage will be quite funny enough as it is, without any unnecessary comic business.

From now onwards, Guglielmo and Don Alfonso must be concealed on the stage. Here is a perfect use for the double scene. Don Alfonso and Guglielmo hide themselves in the passage, and are thus on the stage without being right in the room. At the end of the duet between Ferrando and Fiordiligi (part of which, alas! is left out at Glyndebourne), the inner curtain is pulled across and now that they have drawn even, both officers are compelled to join Don Alfonso in singing *Così fan Tutte,* pointing to the ladies in the audience!

Scene 4

The wedding scene is the culmination of the artificial revue! Here is all the splendour, the finery, the spectacle associated with a grand finale. The whole company is assembled and the knotty argument is concluded amid general rejoicing. The appearance of Despina disguised as the notary is another topical "dig," this time at the expense of the pomposity of the law! All the same, this scene is peaceful and serene. After the turmoils and changes of heart that have gone before, here is the first, and only, real point of repose in the opera. It must be sung with tenderness and sincerity, and it is a pure travesty of the music to pile on the comic business. The exquisite beauty of the music must be left to reveal itself in all its fullness. Even the officers are all seriousness. Ferrando apparently joins in the toasting with enthusiasm, but Guglielmo, aside, bitterly prays that the wine may turn to poison in his glass. The sound of the drums, forecasting the return of the officers, is the signal for terrible and real distress. Too often the girls' desperation is taken as a joke, and they are made to give the impression that they were only waiting for the sound of the drums to go off into false hysterics.

The farce can wait till later when the officers have had their revenge, and demanded the cause of the presence of the notary. Then they reveal the identity of their "Albanian" rivals. Right up to this moment the music is serious, desperately so as far as the ladies are concerned, but once the knot is unravelled there can be universal rejoicing.

The dream is now over, the lovers are reunited, and Don Alfonso has won the wager. It is not unjust for him to claim that the men are wiser for their experience.

IV

DIE ZAUBERFLÖTE

DIE ZAUBERFLÖTE
(The Magic Flute)

Grand Opera in Two Acts, by Emanuel Schikaneder.[1]

Sarastro	Bass
Tamino	Tenor
Orator	Bass
First Priest	(Speaking part)
Second Priest	Tenor
Third Priest	(Speaking part)
Queen of the Night	Soprano
Pamina, her daughter	Soprano
First, Second and Third Ladies . . .	Soprani
Papageno	Bass
An old Woman (Papagena) . . .	Soprano
Monostatos, a Blackamoor . . .	Tenor
First, Second and Third Slaves .	(Speaking parts)

Priests, Slaves and Attendants

The Three Boys (Soprani) and the Armed Men (Tenor and Bass) were not mentioned in the original announcement: in the case of the Three Boys, because these parts were written for, and played by, boys and not women.[2]

The opera was first produced in Vienna on September 30th, 1791.

[1] For a discussion of the question of the authorship of the text of the opera, *see* Jahn, vol. II, page 762, Komorzynski, page 122. These authorities attribute the text to Schikaneder, whereas Dent, page 358, attributes it to Giesecke, a member of Schikaneder's company, and author of "Oberon."

[2] Jahn, vol. II, page 793.

Synopsis of the Story

Act I

Scene 1. *A Rocky Pass*

Tamino, a Prince, runs on to the stage pursued by a serpent, and collapses in a faint. The Three Ladies, the attendants of the Queen of the Night, appear and kill the serpent. They admire the sleeping Prince, and go to tell the Queen of the Night of his arrival. Papageno, the Bird-catcher, comes, and when Tamino awakes, pretends that it was he who killed the serpent. For this lie he is rewarded by the Three Ladies with a padlock for his mouth, a stone instead of the cake, and water instead of the wine which he usually receives in exchange for his birds. The Ladies hand Tamino a picture of the Queen's daughter, with whom he at once falls in love. The Queen herself then appears and tells him that he has been chosen to rescue Pamina from the clutches of the wicked Sarastro. The Ladies give Tamino the Magic Flute, a present from the Queen, to help him in his task. They also remove the lock from Papageno's mouth and give him the Magic Bells, for he is to accompany Tamino, and the Three Boys will escort them to Sarastro's castle.

Scene 2. *Pamina's Boudoir*

Monostatos, the black slave, drags in Pamina, who sinks down helplessly on the couch. Monostatos's intention to assault her is thwarted by the arrival of Papageno. He is at first frightened off by Monostatos, and Monostatos by him, but Papageno recovers himself and returns to tell Pamina of Tamino, who is in love with her, and will come to rescue her.

Scene 3. *Courtyard of the Temple*

Tamino is led in by the Three Boys, and looks around him at the three doors of the Temple. He tries the first two, but is rebuffed. From the third door the Orator emerges, who disillusions him about Sarastro, and tells him that he must put away all thoughts of hatred from his heart before he can win Pamina.

DIE ZAUBERFLÖTE

Tamino, left alone, plays on his Flute, and hears Papageno's pipes answering him. He goes off to find Papageno, who then comes in with Pamina, with whom he is trying to escape. Monostatos and the slaves stop them, but the Magic Bells bewitch the slaves. Trumpets herald the approach of Sarastro, to whom Pamina confesses that she was attempting to escape. Monostatos leads in Tamino, and Sarastro orders that Tamino and Papageno be led off to undergo their trials of initiation.

Act II

Scene 1. *The Temple*

Sarastro tells the assembled Priests that Tamino is destined to be his successor as head of the order of Priests of the Gods, Isis and Osiris.

Scene 2. *A Vault of the Temple*

Tamino and Papageno are enjoined by the Priests to keep silence. The Three Ladies appear and attempt to make them break their vow.

Scene 3. *A Garden*

Pamina is asleep and Monostatos again attempts to assault her. He is driven off by the Queen, who gives her daughter a dagger with which to kill Sarastro. She is in despair to know what to do, when Sarastro himself appears, and tells her to put thoughts of revenge away from her.

Scene 4. *A Hall in the Temple*

Tamino and Papageno are led in by the Orator for their second trial of silence. An old woman appears with a glass of water for Papageno. Just as she is about to tell him her name, she disappears in a clap of thunder. The Three Boys now return with the Magic Flute and Bells, and a table with food and drink for Papageno. Pamina comes in, and as Tamino will not speak to her, she talks of death as the only release from her misery.

Scene 5. *The Temple*

The Priests sing a hymn to Isis and Osiris. Tamino and

Pamina are led in, and told by Sarastro to bid farewell to each other, although they are to meet again.

Scene 6. *A Garden*

Papageno longs for a wife, and the old woman reappears, and offers to marry him. Just as she tells him that her name is Papagena and throws off her old clothes, she is led off by the Priest.

Scene 7. *Another Garden*

Pamina is rescued from attempting suicide by the Three Boys.

Scene 8. *Gateway of the Temple*

Two armed men guard the gates of the Temple, and Tamino and Pamina together undergo the ordeals of fire and water.

Scene 9. *A Garden*

Papageno attempts suicide, but is rescued by the Three Boys, who bring Papagena, with whom he is finally united.

Scene 10. *Outside the Temple*

The Queen, with the Three Ladies and Monostatos, attempt to make an assault upon the Temple.

Scene 11. *The Temple*

Tamino and Pamina, having undergone all the trials, are brought together, and join with Sarastro and the Priests in a chorus of praise to the Gods.

THE OPERA

THE music of Mozart's last opera needs no elaborate explanations. It has an immediate appeal, but its appeal is immeasurably enhanced by a true understanding of the meaning of the story of the opera. In this chapter I have tried to set out my own ideas as to the meaning of *Die Zauberflöte*, and to discuss the proper approach to the opera, with particular reference to its effective production on the stage.

I have included a note on Emanuel Schikaneder,[1] because it appears that the details of his life and work have never been published in English, and particularly because some knowledge of his theatre is essential to a proper appreciation of the opera.

Die Zauberflöte stands apart from the other operas of Mozart which have been considered. They are all straightforward, and do not in any sense reach up towards the sublime. A certain thesis is developed in each, and their immortality is due to the fact that those theses transcend all ages. In them the characters are, for the most part, deep and penetrating studies of humanity. Circumstances change with the advance of civilization, but there are qualities and faults in the human make-up which occur in every age, and consequently the characters are just as real to-day as ever they were. The interest of these operas therefore is primarily human, but compared with *Die Zauberflöte*, they are "of the earth, earthy."

This opera was written for the popular theatre of

[1] *See* Appendix.

141

Emanuel Schikaneder. Apart from the fact that Schikaneder was a fellow Freemason, it seems extraordinary, on the face of it, that Mozart should have accepted his commission to write music for a magic entertainment. The type of magic show which *Die Zauberflöte* was presumably intended to be was nothing new, and all that concerned Schikaneder was that there should be a popular part for himself, that there should be plenty of opportunity for the use of animals, and that the music, particularly that allotted to himself, should be as popular and above all as German as possible. The whole plan of entertainment (for at this stage it can scarcely be called an opera) was to be worked out according to a well-established recipe, and Schikaneder of course knew that the name of Mozart would greatly add to the popular appeal of the work. This was the task which faced Mozart—to write incidental pieces of music, in the manner of the Singspiel, for a transitory entertainment.

How is it possible that this entertainment, starting from such uncertain beginnings, and written with an eye to a particular company of players, and to suit a particular audience, should have become immortal? It is true that at one time, at any rate in England, *Die Zauberflöte* was not generally appreciated, but it seems that to-day it is indispensable to any opera company's repertory. So far as it is possible to judge, it does not appear that this present popularity is but a passing phase, for *Die Zauberflöte* has taken firm root in the popular imagination. It is therefore fair to refer to it as immortal, and the reason for this immortality is that it contains a universal philosophy, expressed in a medium that is accessible to all.

Die Zauberflöte brilliantly fulfilled Schikaneder's commission; it was a magic entertainment turned out in the

prescribed manner, with magic, animals, glorious oppor-
tunities for grandiose effects and a wonderful part for
Schikaneder himself. Above all, this entertainment was
German to the core. If it had done no more than provide
Schikaneder with another successful piece for his theatre,
it would not have survived until to-day, and even Schikaneder himself would have been forgotten. As it was,
Mozart exceeded what was required of him in two respects.
In the first place he infused this magic entertainment with
music such as he had never written before; music that
lifted it right out of its surroundings, and by its sheer
simplicity and directness achieved depth of expression and
sincerity.

This glorious music is surely the supreme achievement
of German Romanticism. Here is none of the cheap senti-
ment which was so great a feature of the later Romantic
Movement. After the formal elegance, then grown dusty,
of the Italian culture of the eighteenth century, here was
the first breath of fresh air. *Die Zauberflöte* is the top of
the pass, the glorious view. Once the pass is reached, and
after that first sight of the view, all else is a decline.
Nothing equals the thrill of that first moment. From
then onwards, the traveller walks down and down, the
beauty of the top of the pass behind him, never to be
experienced again. After *Die Zauberflöte,* the German
Romantic movement is a decline. The composers and
poets of the later years, although fortified by collections of
folk songs, poems and tales, never again achieved the
freshness of the top of the pass.

Secondly, Mozart adapted the story of *Die Zauberflöte*
and made it the vehicle for expressing his ideas upon life
and for glorifying the order of Freemasons. This involved
a fundamental change in the story of the opera, and

accounts for the glaring inconsistencies which mar the plot. There are those who maintain that the story of the opera is not inconsistent with itself, but it seems clear upon analysis that the story was in fact changed in the middle of the composition of the opera. As first planned, the opera would no doubt have told the story of the rescue of the stolen Pamina by Tamino, who overcame the wicked tyrant Sarastro with the aid of the Magic Flute. As it stands the opera is consistent with this view of the story during the first two scenes. The handsome Prince Tamino is rescued from death by the agents of the Queen, who is portrayed as an innocent and bereft mother. Tamino is charged by her with the task of rescuing her daughter, and is supplied, by the Queen, with the Magic Flute to help him to overcome Sarastro. The first appearance of Pamina also confirms this view. She is shown as a prisoner, ill-treated by a black slave, and she attempts to escape when she hears that her mother has sent a messenger to rescue her.

After this scene the whole plot changes. At once when the Orator appears, it becomes apparent that Sarastro is not the wicked tyrant at all, but that he is the great human benefactor, who has rescued Pamina from the clutches of a selfish mother. Thereafter Sarastro and his priests appear as the representatives of good, and the Queen and her attendants become the representatives of evil.

The reason for the change, assuming that one took place, has been attributed to various circumstances. The conventional theory is that in the middle of its composition, Marinelli produced an opera based on the same story, and therefore Schikaneder and Mozart were compelled to alter the plan of *Die Zauberflöte,* and give it a serious ending. It seems impossible to believe that Schikaneder would have been troubled in the least by the thought that his work might be taken for a copy of something produced by Marinelli. Throughout his career he freely adapted the ideas of others for his own use, and therefore this explanation of the alteration of *Die Zauberflöte* is insufficient. The real reason which led to the change must remain a matter for speculation, although the sources from which Schikaneder and Mozart drew the idea for the original, and for the revised story, can be clearly traced.[1]

On the whole, it seems more probable that the change was due to Schikaneder and Mozart alone, and not to any external circumstances. A study of the opera seems to lead inevitably to this conclusion. It is surely no exaggeration to say that, as he worked, the significance of the subject deepened for Mozart, and he saw in it more and more the possibilities which it offered for expressing all those things which to him were most sacred. Through Sarastro and his priests he could glorify for ever the order of Freemasons, and the simplicity of their music lends deep sincerity to their message. If this view be correct, and if it be true that Mozart changed his whole conception of *Die Zauberflöte* in the middle of its composition, it seems curious that he did not re-write the opening scenes to make them conform to his higher view of the work. It may have been that there was no time at his disposal to alter what he had written before the opera was required for performance.

Once the possibility of this wider view of the magic story had occurred to Mozart, every feature of it fell into its place, and assumed for him a hitherto unexpected

[1] For a full account of this subject the reader is referred to Dent, chapter XIII, and to Komorzynski, pages 109 *et seq.*

significance. In the result *Die Zauberflöte* resembles a parable. At first sight, it is a simple magic story, exactly what was required by Schikaneder. Underneath the surface, however, this simple magic story has a depth of meaning which remains to-day as significant as ever it was to Mozart himself.

THE CHARACTERS

Each element of the opera, and each character, when examined, seems to fit in with this view. The Magic Flute itself, on the face of it an ordinary property in a magic entertainment, is surely conclusive evidence that the story underwent a change. This Flute emanates from the Queen, given to Tamino to help him to overcome Sarastro, and yet it becomes, as the opera proceeds, a touchstone for Tamino, a sure guide to him throughout all the trials, and a solace in adversity. Is this a mere magic contrivance? Rather has it become a symbol, almost a sacred rite, whereby Tamino may commune with the Divine. Throughout his trials, when oppressed by the petty things of the world, when faced with jealousy or hatred, it is the Flute which comes to his aid, and reminds him of the ideals of humanity and love which Sarastro and his priests put before him as life's goal.

What of Papageno, a part devised for Schikaneder himself, whose music was to be as popular as possible, and who was to provide the comic relief in the midst of the terrors of the Temple? Again, on the face of it, Papageno fulfils these functions, and yet how much deeper is the significance which the part assumes in the higher view of the opera. Papageno, "Naturmensch," as he describes him-

self, is the personification of the flesh, to whom all the
higher spiritual values in life mean nothing. He is incap-
able of understanding the meaning of the trials, and he can
never aspire to the perfect life. Throughout the opera he
provides a complete contrast to Tamino, whose manly
courage and spiritual triumph would not be seen so
clearly, were it not for the background provided by
Papageno. It is true that he achieves his desires, such as
they are, without passing through any of the trials successfully, but his desires and their ultimate fulfilment are
limited to the material things of life. Papageno is a
pathetic and unsophisticated, but certainly not a purely
farcical figure.[1]

The Three Boys are another indication of the change of
story. They are mentioned in the first place as the servants of the Queen, who will conduct Tamino and Papageno to the Temple and, presumably, assist in the rescue
of Pamina. And yet their later appearances reveal them as
the agents of Sarastro, in each case furthering his purpose.
From them Tamino and Papageno receive back the Magic
Flute and Bells, which have been taken away. By them
Pamina and Papageno in turn are rescued from suicide,
and brought back to the life which Sarastro has prepared
for them. Instead of being merely part of the usual trap-
pings of a magic entertainment, they have become, in a
sense, divine messengers. In the production at Glyndebourne, already mentioned, the celestial character of the

[1] In the Glyndebourne production of the opera in 1935 Papageno was
made to "gag" in English. The idea was to re-create something of the
atmosphere of Schikaneder's performance of the part. If the idea was a
good one, in practice it was ineffective. The same phrases, not particularly
funny in themselves, were repeated at each performance, and there was
therefore no original humour in the result. Schikaneder himself probably
introduced all kinds of topical jokes, but a dull repetition of prepared
phrases did not achieve the same effect.

Three Boys was emphasized by keeping them behind a gauze veil. Each time they appeared they were thus seen only vaguely, as if they were figures in some dream or fantasy. It is to be observed that they have no individual existence. They always sing together and should therefore always move in a group upon the stage.

Tamino himself begins the opera as the ordinary Prince, the standard character of the fairy story, who rescues and, of course, marries the Princess in distress. He falls in love with her picture, another familiar feature of a fairy story, and sets off at once with high ideas for the overthrow of the wicked Sarastro. In his long interview with the Orator he is shown as the obstinate and impetuous youth who is satisfied that his ideas are right. But here at once his rôle in the opera has changed. In contrast to his impetuosity, the patience and restraint of the Orator show that Sarastro and his order are not the wicked tyrants which they were at first portrayed to be. From now on Tamino appears to be convinced of his mistake. At the end of his conversation with the priest he has ceased to question, and has come to accept the authority of Sarastro. All his arrogance has gone, and he willingly submits himself to the trials which Sarastro imposes upon him. He humbles himself, and prepares to make himself worthy for the higher life, worthy to grasp the hand of friendship which the Orator has promised shall be extended to him, worthy in the end to win Pamina and to succeed Sarastro as head of the order of the priests of Isis and Osiris.

The trials to which he must submit himself, and the rites of the priestly order, represent the ceremonies of initiation of the Freemasons, as is shown by the continual reference throughout the opera to the mystic number three. Tamino is no ordinary fairy prince. He becomes the novice, dedicating his life to the sacred priesthood of the gods, a calling of which he shows himself to be worthy.

This Priesthood cannot have played any part in the original conception of the story. When first mentioned by the Queen, Sarastro is spoken of as a villain and the impression is that he is a neighbouring ruler who has carried Pamina off to his Castle. Tamino and Papageno ask the Three Ladies how they shall find Sarastro's castle (Burg). But as the possibilities of the story developed in Mozart's mind, the Priests came to play an important part. They are the initiates of the order, and have themselves passed through the trials and achieved that peace of mind and serenity which is Tamino's goal. In the opera they are in the background, imparting an atmosphere of dignity and peace to the scenes in the Temple.

In the final form of the opera the Queen and the Three Ladies become the representatives of Evil, definitely opposed to all that Sarastro and his Priests uphold. No such significance attached to them originally, for at the beginning the Queen appears as the sorrowing mother, robbed of her daughter, and the Ladies as her attendants. In the second Act, however, it is the Ladies who become the temptresses, trying to induce Tamino to break his vow of silence; and in the penultimate scene of all, the Queen and the Ladies make an ineffective assault upon the Temple. It is interesting to see how the Queen's importance dwindles as the opera proceeds. At the beginning she appears as the great Queen who dominates the whole region. Papageno has his livelihood from her, but she is too great for him ever to have seen. Tamino at once accepts her commission to rescue her daughter, and does not for a moment question her authority. At this stage it is clear that she was intended to be the central figure of the opera, and that the conclusion of the story would see her daughter safely returned, rescued from the evil-doer's clutches. By the time she next appears, she has already lost all her character, and her injunctions to Pamina are the backbitings of an embittered spirit. At her third and last appearance she has ceased to be effective at all, and her attack on the Temple serves, by contrast, to emphasize the glory of Tamino's triumph, and the greatness of Sarastro and the Priests.

One more simple instance of the higher significance of the story is to be found in Papageno's duet with Pamina in the first Act. He finds her alone and tells her of Tamino, who has fallen in love with her picture and who will come to win her as his bride. In the magic story it is natural that they should join together in a song in praise of love. Mozart, however, has infused their simple, almost doggerel words with such a sense of divinity as to take the duet right out of the atmosphere of a fairy story. The result is a prayer, expressing the perfect conception of man's love for woman, for through love alone can man approach the infinite.

THE PRODUCTION

Apart from the reference to Isis and Osiris, there is nothing in *Die Zauberflöte* to tie it down either as to time or place. Isis and Osiris fix the scene as Egypt, and so it was evidently intended by the authors. There has, however, been an over-insistence on the Egyptian atmosphere in the manner in which the opera has been staged, and this has tended to obscure its real significance. The message of Sarastro is thus made remote and unconvincing, and only dimly penetrates through the atmosphere of the "East."

The only essential feature of the scenery and dresses must be consistency of style, but it is suggested that the opera is better staged in settings that are general and not reminiscent of any particular age or civilization. The meaning of the opera is too wide to be confined to one epoch. A break from Egypt is a welcome feature in a modern production of *Die Zauberflöte,* and will achieve its purpose if it serves to show the opera in a new light, and so revives interest in it. The Glyndebourne settings and costumes for the opera achieved this generality, and showed it against a background that had no reference to reality.

On the other hand, there must be mentioned the revival of *Die Zauberflöte* at Covent Garden in 1938, for which Schinkel's famous Egyptian settings were used. Here was at any rate a welcome consistency of effect, sadly lacking in some modern Egyptian settings of the opera. These vast and spacious scenes suited the enormous stage at Covent Garden to perfection, and a great dignity of effect was achieved.

Act I

Scene 1

The opening page of the opera, with the entry and collapse of Tamino, is most dramatic and even terrible from the musical point of view. The chromatic progressions, which are the chief characteristics of the music, are singularly expressive of mortal anguish, and the music is written in the minor mode, suggesting tragedy. Tamino runs on to the stage, breathlessly cries for help and collapses from exhaustion. He is closely followed by a serpent, and the indication is that he should be in hunting costume with a bow, but no arrows, thereby adding to his plight. "Serpent" was substituted for "ferocious lion" in the

151

manuscript, and some significance may attach to this, for to the Freemasons, as also in the Bible, the serpent was the symbol of evil. Unfortunately this opening scene is seldom convincingly staged, for at least two reasons. In the first place there are often several exits available for Tamino, and yet he falls down without escaping by them. Secondly, the serpent is far from terrifying, and is usually no more than a cardboard animal pushed on from the wings.

To make the scene dramatically effective two methods are suggested. Either it must be apparent that Tamino has entered the stage by the only gap in the rocks, leaving himself no other possible means of escape from the serpent, or else there must be three entrances. He then comes in by the first, pursued by a serpent, and tries the other two entrances in turn, only to find his way barred by two other serpents. The Three Ladies then each have a serpent to kill. Sometimes it is sought to add to the dramatic effect of the scene by making one or two frightened figures run across the stage during the introduction. This procedure has precisely the opposite effect, for it makes it clear that Tamino could have followed them off the stage.

The serpent is certainly a difficult problem, and the way in which it is presented must depend upon the resources of the individual theatre. However it is done, it is essential that the serpent should be clearly seen, and if possible that it should be large. Tamino subsequently turns out to be a courageous individual, and it must be apparent that he is in the grip of a real danger to make his collapse convincing. Surely Schikaneder would have spared no pains to produce a realistic serpent!

If the second course suggested is followed, and there are three entrances, as soon as Tamino has collapsed, one Lady

appears at each entrance and kills her respective serpent.
The Ladies must not appear (or be seen) a moment before
Tamino collapses, or the dramatic effect of their "Stirb
Ungeheuer" is spoilt. They must be made as attractive as
possible, for their music is essentially feminine and above
all Viennese. Only at the beginning is it at all pompous.
There is even so a certain sense of humour in their pomposity, particularly in the boisterous accompaniment of
trumpets and drums which heralds their entrance. But as
soon as they set eyes on Tamino, their natural musical
language comes out, and reveals them in their true light.
They entirely abandon themselves to their feminine in-
stincts, and vie with each other in praising Tamino's
beauty. Of all the characters in the opera, these Ladies are
surely the most ill-treated. Why is it that they are always
dressed up to look like Britannia[1] in mourning at the
village carnival? Surely it is time that producers considered the Three Ladies more seriously, and paid more
attention to the important part which they play in the
opera, particularly from the musical point of view. Performances of *Die Zauberflöte* are easily praised or condemned by the qualities of the singing of Tamino or
Sarastro, but the difficult ensembles of the Three Ladies
are a surer guide to the care which has been bestowed
upon the preparation of the opera. If *Die Zauberflöte*
is to be produced properly, and not merely as a patch-
work of inconsistencies, the Three Ladies must cease to be
figures of fun.

As soon as they are gone, the music commences with
the introduction to Papageno's song. Tamino slowly wakes

[1] The costumes used at Glyndebourne for the Three Ladies perfectly
underlined their character, and their flippantly suggested hunting habit
added to the probability of their carrying spears.

up, and speaks while this music is played. The impression to be created is that the sound of Papageno's pipes has roused him, and realizing that someone is approaching, he hides behind the rocks and watches. Papageno's song is a typical "Auftrittslied," a song belonging in style to the German "Singspiel." The words are straightforward, and introduce the character to the audience without any ado. He does not give his name, but otherwise Papageno precisely describes his character and outlook on life in this simple song. It is not perhaps out of place to mention that the song is marked "Andante," and that Papageno must at all costs play his pipes himself. Even if it is difficult for him to time his pipings accurately, what is thereby lost in musical exactitude is more than made up by the gain in realism. Tamino has watched Papageno closely during his song, at first perhaps not without apprehension. At the end, therefore, he emerges somewhat hesitantly and addresses the bird-catcher. It is a mistake for Tamino to have been off the stage altogether during the song, and then to walk in and approach Papageno casually as an old friend.

Until the end of Tamino's picture song, when the Queen appears, no change of scene is necessary. The rocky pass need only occupy the front portion of the stage, and there is then ample room for the Queen of the Night to appear behind. She must appear and disappear to the accompaniment of thunder and lightning, and it must not be apparent how or whence she appears. She stands upon a rock, or seems rather to grow out of the side of the mountain. The stage is darkened for her song, and it is clear that she is a personality apart from the rest of the opera. Her formal music rather serves to emphasize her character of other-worldliness. She must display no signs of being a human being, and should stand absolutely still and erect during her song.

When she is gone, the rocky pass is shown once more, and the scene is not changed until Pamina's boudoir. The Quintet is at once comic and serious. Comic as far as Papageno is concerned until his padlock is removed, and comic again when he asks if the Ladies have no present for him. For the ensembles, the music is serious and almost moralizing. The Ladies, particularly when they present the flute, appear again in their seductive feminine rôle, and take their leave of the men in the most delicately affectionate manner.

Scene 2

The first substantial change of scene shows Pamina's boudoir, within the precincts of Sarastro's domain. Perhaps it is as well to start this scene with the Trio, and cut out all the dialogue between the slaves that precedes it. This particular dialogue adds nothing to the plot, nor does it lead up to anything which follows. It is true that Monostatos orders the slaves to prepare chains for Pamina, but he calls out for them during the Trio, and so the dialogue is redundant. The entry of Papageno must be so arranged that he does not see Monostatos until the actual moment when both of them sing "Hu, das ist der Teufel." Then they both back off the stage—their steps in time with the music—and bump into each other as they reach the exit. They creep off the stage on tiptoe, rather than run, and sing their words rather than shriek. The music is delicate, and their fear is such as to render them almost speechless.

The duet between Pamina and Papageno is unusual, in that the two young people unite in the praise of love, but their love is not mutual; they do not feel it for each other.

They are praising love in the abstract, and there must therefore be no coyness or false embarrassment between them. The behaviour of Pamina and Papageno in this duet must be such, that it never enters the mind that there is any subtlety in the words they sing, or that they bear any but their face meaning.

Scene 3

The Three Boys lead in Tamino, and both their music and their words at once introduce them as agents of Sarastro, no longer, apparently, servants of the Queen. They enjoin Tamino to be steadfast, patient and discreet. This may not strictly be the first appearance of the Three Boys, for although there is nothing to indicate it in the text, in some productions they are made to walk across the back of the stage at the end of Scene 1, when the Three Ladies tell the men that Three Boys will show them the way to Sarastro's castle. This illustrates at once the difficulties with which the producer of the opera is faced by reason of the change of the story. As has already been mentioned, these Three Boys start by being messengers of the Queen, but they at once change their rôle and become agents of Sarastro. The effect of walking the Boys across the stage when they are first mentioned is charming, and one which a producer would clearly be reluctant to miss; on the other hand, this appearance definitely serves to emphasize the inconsistency of the story in this respect. Therefore it is submitted that the better course is to wait until they lead Tamino into the Temple, and not to bring them on to the stage at the behest of the Three Ladies in the earlier scene. Of course this method leaves Tamino and Papageno high and dry on the stage in the earlier scene, for the principal object of having the Boys is to enable the men to follow them off the stage, presumably setting out on their journey to the castle. When the Boys have left him alone Tamino surveys the Temple. There are three doors before him, and he boldly approaches each in turn, challenging Sarastro. In this scene, both here and at the end, music off the stage is required. As he approaches the first two doors Tamino is rebuffed by a hidden cry of "Zurück." It should be clear that these cries are coming from behind the particular door in each case, and the word "Zurück" should come out like a thunderbolt. It may be that it is difficult to make singers heard from behind the scenes, for these cries are inclined to pass unnoticed. One excellent device, seen at Sadler's Wells, in 1937, may be adopted, which serves to emphasize these cries. The two first doors are mere portals, with no actual door, and at the crucial moment they are lit up for a brief second. This leaves no doubt that the cry is coming from behind the particular door. On paper, the cries seem to be telling enough. Tamino's challenging approach to each door is accompanied by a delicate phrase, which sets the time for Tamino's paces, and then "Zurück!" is bellowed out decisively to the accompaniment of straightforward chords. The Orator emerges from the third door, and his calm and dignified music, not untinged with warmth, is contrasted with Tamino's impetuous outbursts. The contrast is emphasized if the Orator stands still in the doorway during the duet, towering over Tamino.

For Tamino's flute song—which incidentally is marked Andante—the stage is darkened, and gauze curtains across the back may suggest a wood as the background. The song is directed to an audience of animals and birds, who move when the flute plays. The best method of dealing with these animals would appear to be to use lights. Pairs of green eyes, which move about with the flute music, might be seen in the wood. In this way the impression of magic attraction could be more effectively created than by the presence of real animals. This is the first use of the Magic Flute, and its music is comparatively simple and devoid of virtuoso passages. Benedikt Schack, the first Tamino, was a composer and also a flautist of no mean achievement, and in this song, and in the other flute music, Mozart no doubt had him in mind. Throughout the opera the Flute only plays when Tamino is not singing, so that Schack evidently played the flute music himself.

Is not this first use of the Flute conclusive proof of the change of the story? If it were merely a magic weapon, Tamino could have overcome the Temple with it, and all resistance would be broken down in face of its bewitching music. But in the final form of the story it plays no such part. Tamino is here left alone, in a strange place, with unknown difficulties to encounter. He has been left mystified by the obscure answers of the Priest, and naturally turns to his Flute for comfort and support. He meditates upon his position, and quietly prepares himself for his mission to the accompaniment of soothing music.

At the end of the song, the wood disappears and the stage is lit up again for the final scene of the Act. Pamina and Papageno run in followed by Monostatos. Here is the first use of the Magic Bells. Their melody is simple and essentially Austrian in character, not altogether unrelated to the Tyrolese yodel! Papageno cannot, of course, play their music himself, but it is better that his bells should be mounted on a frame, and by striking them with a stick he gives some impression of playing the tune. The slaves are entirely bewitched, and dance off the stage automatically. Their retreat is not comic. They are bound by a magic spell and are no longer in control of their limbs. They must all dance together, stiffly like marionettes.

The remainder of the Act is straightforward, but a word is perhaps not out of place on the conduct of Tamino and Pamino. This is their first meeting, and although they sing "Es schling mein Arm sich um ihn (sie) her," it is wrong for them to embrace. Their love for each other is mystic, and in no sense physical. Throughout the opera they should do no more than hold hands rather formally. A homely embrace is alien to their relationship, which is essentially spiritual, symbolizing the ideal.

Act II

In this Act there are no less than eleven episodes for which a change of scene is required, and before considering each episode, some definite method of approach to the scenic problems involved must be adopted. For the three scenes in the Temple, 1, 5 and 11, the same scenery may be used. In each of these scenes the stage is required to be full, so that the scenery may be set at the back of the stage, and the other scenery mounted in front of it. The rest of the scenes, except 8, can all be played in a small space, so that a backcloth is all that is necessary for them. Only Scene 8, the ordeals of fire and water, requires more elaborate treatment.

Scene 1

The Act opens with the March of the Priests and Sarastro's great song "O Isis und Osiris." This music, and also the Chorus of the Priests which follows in Scene 5, is essentially solemn and ceremonial. The March is marked "Andante," and the Song and Chorus "Adagio," and these three together, in a supreme effort to create an effect of great seriousness, are often so dragged as to leave an impression of intolerable boredom associated with Sarastro and his order. The music itself will be solemn enough if played normally, and an effort to make it more so will detract from its solemnity and make it dull. The effect of the entry of the Priests during the March is greatly enhanced at Glyndebourne by raising the curtain on a dark stage, and then slowly lighting the Priests as they file into their places, reserving the full light until the end of the March.

Sarastro, in the final form of the opera, is the great human benefactor, opposed to the Queen, the inhuman champion of evil. He made a brief appearance at the end of the first Act, but here amid his Priests he is first seen in all his grandeur. He solemnly tells the assembled Priests that Tamino is chosen to be his successor, and invites them to signify their assent while the mystic "Dreimalige Akkord" is sounded. According to the stage directions, the Priests each have a trumpet, upon which they are supposed to sound the solemn notes. In practice, it is perhaps better to deviate from the directions and leave the Priests without trumpets. It is always patently obvious that the "Akkord" is not played by them but by the orchestra, and the handling of the trumpets, before and after the "Akkord," is liable to be reminiscent of an arms drill parade. However, without the trumpets some formal gesture must be made during the "Akkord," or there would be no point in Sarastro's invitation *Haltet ihr ihn für würdig, so folgt meinem Beispiele* ("If you consider him worthy, follow my example"). Before the advent of Dictators the raising of the right arm was the

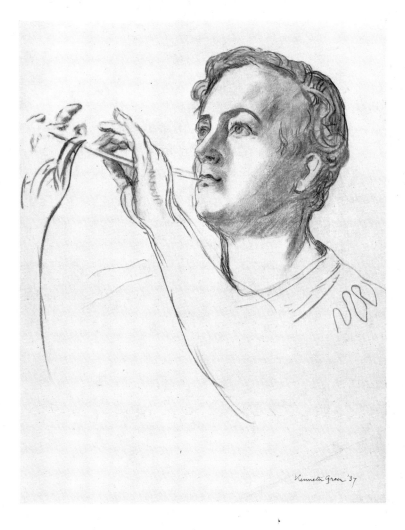

Thorkild Noval as TAMINO in *Die Zauberflöte*
(Glyndebourne)

most effective and solemn gesture for occasions such as this. Now, however, some substitute must be found. In this short scene Sarastro's rôle of guardian of humanity is made abundantly clear. He describes Tamino's qualifications to succeed him as head of the order, and his supreme claim to such honour is not that he is steadfast, nor even that he is a Prince, but simply "Er ist Mensch!"

During the dialogue the solemn chords are played three times. On each occasion all three chords should be sounded, not one by itself. These chords have a definite Masonic significance, and here again the mystic number three is in evidence.

Scene 2

The Priests' solemn warning to Tamino and Papageno to keep silence is at once followed by the arrival of the Three Ladies, who tempt them to break their vow. Observe the subtle way in which they set about their task. They begin with an attempt to frighten them. When this fails, they announce that the Queen is at hand, but this too is of no avail. Then they play their last card, and ask ingenuously, *Warum bist du mit uns so spröde?* ("Why are you so shy with us?") In the end their delicate, seductive and essentially feminine character prevails. If this scene is played in front of some sort of curtain, then the Ladies should appear from behind it, and stay behind the men throughout the scene whispering their threats almost into their ears.

Scene 3

Pamina is asleep on a couch; the stage is dark, and the moon is shining on her face. The moon is referred to by

Monostatos, but the stage must in any event be dark and sombre for the appearance of the Queen. Monostatos, with his black features, should not be too clearly seen during his song. The whole impression created by his music is one of weirdness, as it were the accompaniment to the midnight prowlings of a burglar. He circles round his victim, getting closer and closer until he is disturbed by the Queen. The Queen must appear, as before, without it being apparent whence or how she arrived. She is more human, more approachable in this scene than before, but even so it is better to keep her apart as a mysterious and aloof personality. It is a mistake therefore for her to embrace Pamina or even to approach her during her song. Pamina is sorry for her mother, and apparently loves her deeply, but she has seen too much of Sarastro's humanity to accept her mother's view of him and his order. The Queen should stand behind Pamina, and throw down the dagger.

In this scene the direct contrast between the Queen and Sarastro is made abundantly clear. The Queen's bitter utterances, exhorting her daughter to revenge, leave Pamina in a state of perturbation. For the moment, her loyalties are divided. She wavers between obedience to her mother and gratitude to Sarastro. When Sarastro appears, he immediately appreciates this mental strife, and his warm counsel of friendship and love win her confidence at once, and restore to her the serenity and peace of mind which her mother has temporarily disturbed.

The dialogue in this scene should be drastically cut. Monostatos' opening speech should be left out, and one word from the Queen, "Zurück!" drives him away, and is all that need separate his song from hers. When the Queen has gone, Sarastro should appear at once. Pamina need not speak, but her face indicates her fears, which are at once allayed by Sarastro's "Ich weiss alles." All the other dialogue should be left out.

Scene 4

The dialogue is essential here in order to make the plot quite clear. This is the second appearance of the Three Boys, who bring back the Flute and Bells and also some food. "When we meet for the third time," they say, "joy will be the reward of your courage." The point of this remark is obscure. Their only other appearances in the opera are the scenes of Pamina's and Papageno's attempted suicides. Perhaps their words are addressed solely to Papageno? The reference is probably to the last scene of all, where they appear as witnesses to Tamino's triumph.

Scenes 5—11

From this point onwards, as appears from the synopsis of the scenes given above, there are considerable inconsistencies in the story. Lert[1] suggests that these may be overcome by altering the order of the scenes. His proposals seem so eminently reasonable that they are worth quoting in full. "In the second Act a change seems to me to be necessary and important. I have a definite feeling that originally Schikaneder and Mozart placed Pamina's suicide scene (7) directly after her rebuke from Tamino and her song 'Ach ich fühl's' (4). The Trio (5) was either introduced later or was originally placed after Pamina's attempted suicide (7). Thus the suicide scene (7) never seems to be necessary or logical, for in the Trio (5) Sarastro has told Pamina: *Ihr werdet froh euch wieder-*

[1] Page 405.

sehen! ('You shall meet again with joy!'), and her frantic
question in the suicide scene *Warum sprach er nicht mit
mir?* ('Why did he not speak to me?') is out of place as
it now stands, for Tamino has just spoken to her in the
Trio (5). The suicide scene (7) follows much more
logically upon Pamina's rebuke from Tamino (4), as the
closing words of her song *So wird Ruh im Tode sein*
('Death will bring peace') lead up to it clearly."

We can therefore arrange the scenes in the following
way: after Pamina's appearance and song "Ach ich fühl's"
(4), the text clearly indicates that Tamino courageously
goes forward, while Papageno cowardly lags behind: in the
lion episode, usually omitted, Tamino is already off the
stage. So on the third blast of the trumpet Tamino
hurries off, and Papageno calls after him as he goes, *Eile
nur nicht so, wir kommen noch immer zeitig genug, uns
braten zu lassen* ("Don't hurry so, we shall still get there
in time to be roasted"). Then at once, and with the same
scenery we have Scene (6). Papageno's first words in this
scene, *Tamino, willst du mich denn gänzlich verlassen?*
("Tamino, will you abandon me altogether?"), follow on
so logically that one must conclude that originally these
two scenes belonged together. Now we proceed until the
old woman is changed into Papagena and is removed by
the Priest. Then follows the scene of the Three Boys and
Pamina's attempted suicide (7). Papageno's hanging
scene (9), which (according to Löwenfeld) is a parody of
Pamina's suicide scene (7), comes next, and ends with the
union of Papageno and Papagena. Now comes scene (5),
where, after the Chorus, Pamina is led in by the Three
Boys and joins Tamino. The trio (5) thus acquires its
logical position. Now, having disposed of Papageno's
fooling, we can take the sacred trials to their end in one

sweep. After the trio (5) there follow at once the scene with the armed men and the trials of fire and water (8); the appearance of the Queen with the Ladies and Mono- statos (10) and the Finale (11).

Thus the story becomes plain. It is clear that Papageno does not go farther with Tamino; clear that Pamina really has cause for her desperation; and clear that she voluntarily undergoes the trials, not fearing night and death, and thus makes herself worthy to be initiated.

This procedure seems to have everything in its favour. Whether Lert is right in assuming that the scenes were originally in a different order does not matter. The im- portant point is to make the opera convincing on the modern stage, and Lert's suggested alterations remove all the inconsistencies inherent in the present order of the scenes. Further, his proposals do not involve any cuts or modifications of the music.

Little need be said of the remaining scenes. Papageno's two episodes are not entirely comic. Surely there is an element of tragedy in this primitive "Naturmensch" striving to find a wife. For him a wife after his own form represents the only goal in life. With a wife at his side he will find earthly peace, and face the world with a brave heart. Pure farce in these scenes is out of place.

Their trials finally overcome, Tamino and Pamina are received by the assembled company of Priests, and the opera concludes with a glorious chorus in praise of Sarastro. This is a moment of triumph. Tamino, like Walther in the *Mastersingers*, has won his bride after severe tests of his prowess and integrity. Formal pseudo-Egyptian dances, such as sometimes accompany the scene, are out of place. An impressive tableau is all that is required, and the pro- ducer should aim at presenting a gloriously lit spectacle, brighter than anything which has been seen before. No action is necessary, for music alone is adequate to express this supreme service of thanksgiving.

The music, the story, the spectacle—all these are important elements in *Die Zauberflöte*, but they recede into the background in the face of its spiritual message. This opera can be an inspiration. Courage, self-control, love, these are the qualities of the higher life to which Tamino and Pamina are introduced by Sarastro. Without these, life is empty, and there is no joy in achievement, no harmony between men. Without these, men cannot have peace of mind, and without peace of mind no material benefits can avail him. Sarastro's leadership changes Tamino's life. At the end he has won moral strength, and his admission to the order of priests signifies his achievement of a new standard of life.

How near, how fascinatingly near to the greatest exposition of the conduct of the perfect life is this teaching of Sarastro. How interesting the speculation that Mozart himself may have regarded this opera as his great opportunity to glorify that teaching. Here was a subject fit to call forth the very essence of his soul, and the fact that the true meaning of the story lies beneath the surface helped him. Here was no self-conscious setting of a sacred theme, no strained piety. On the surface a magic opera written for a popular theatre, beneath a message of hope. In a word, a parable.

There is great danger in attributing motives to the authors of the great masterpieces of the world. Too much meaning has been read into the works of the immortal, and modern analysis may overburden verses that bore none but their face meaning for those who penned them. This view of *Die Zauberflöte* is open to the same criticism. Nevertheless, a work of art survives through the ages only because each generation, each individual admirer, reads into it a personal message and derives from it a benefit that others may not see. This, therefore, is but a personal message of *Die Zauberflöte*.

At the present time it is not surprising that *Die Zauberflöte* should win favour. In a world overcome by fear, man searches for peace of mind. Sarastro expounds the Christian doctrine in a new form. By unselfishness and love, and by devoting themselves to a higher life, Sarastro and his priests have banished fear from their hearts. Their message finds universal acceptance in a troubled world, and Mozart's music is the vehicle which cannot fail to make their message real.

APPENDIX

LORENZO DA PONTE
(1749–1838)

Lorenzo da Ponte, who wrote the libretti for Mozart's Italian operas, was born in 1749 at Ceneda, the son of an Italian Jew named Conegliano. In 1763 the whole family was received into the Catholic Church, and thereupon, as was apparently the custom of the time, they assumed the name of the Bishop who performed the ceremony. Lorenzo da Ponte, as he now became, led an adventurous life, becoming a priest in 1773, and later seeking his fortune as a poet in Venice, Treviso, Gorizia, Dresden, and eventually in Vienna. His *Memoirs* tell the story of these years in great detail. They were not written until years later, and the passage of time probably lent wings to his memory. But however exaggerated or distorted his *Memoirs* may be, it is abundantly clear from them that he was for ever escaping from his creditors, or from scandals of one sort or another.

He came to Vienna in 1781,[1] with an introduction to the famous composer Salieri, through whose influence he eventually obtained the post of poet to the Imperial Theatre. He first met Mozart in 1783, and wrote for him the libretti of *Le Nozze di Figaro*, *Don Giovanni* and *Così fan Tutte*. The last of these was produced in 1790, and Da Ponte in that year went to Trieste, having fallen out with his Viennese protectors. He there married an English girl, with whom he went to London. In 1805, however, he was obliged to flee to America to escape his creditors.

There he seems to have led just as hazardous a life as before, until he eventually settled down in New York teaching Italian, and furthering a knowledge of Italian literature, until his death in 1838. He describes in his *Memoirs* (vol. II, page 75) the thrill which he had in 1825, when Vincenzo Garcia visited New York with an Italian company of singers and performed Rossini's *Barber of Seville*. Da Ponte takes credit for having suggested to Garcia

[1] Professor Dent writes: "Da Ponte passed through Vienna in December 1780, on the way to Dresden. The date of his settling in Vienna is uncertain, but not later than early in 1782."

that he should vary the repertory by adding *Don Giovanni,* and also for having found him a singer for the part of Ottavio. The impression gained from the *Memoirs* is that these were the only two operas which Garcia's company performed in New York. In fact, however, during 1825 and 1826, many other Italian operas were given by the company, and particularly Rossini's *Tancredi, Otello* and *Cenerentola.* Garcia had a special interest in Rossini, for he was a famous tenor as well as manager of the company, and it was he who had first sung Count Almaviva in the *Barber of Seville.* Most unfortunately, Da Ponte gives no account of these performances.

EMANUEL SCHIKANEDER [1]
(1751–1812)

1751. Johann Emanuel Schikaneder, Mozart's collaborator in *Die Zauberflöte*, was born at Regensburg.

1773. Joined Schopf's German travelling company, and became actor, singer and producer.

1776. Married Eleonore Ardtim, a fellow member of Schopf's theatrical company.
Schikaneder and his wife left Schopf, and joined Moser's company as juvenile leads.
Triumphant appearance as Hamlet in Munich led to Schikaneder being engaged by the Munich theatre.

1778. Purchased Moser's Company, and thus, at the early age of 27, became director of his own company.
The repertory of the company at this time included plays of Shakespeare (particularly *Hamlet*, in the title rôle of which Schikaneder repeated his Munich success; also *Macbeth* and *King Lear*) and the early dramas of Lessing, Goethe and Schiller; operas of Gluck, Mozart and Haydn, and also many examples of the early German Singspiel.

1780. Mozart first met Schikaneder, when the latter's company. was at Salzburg.

1781–2. Schikaneder's company in Graz, where he had great success with open-air performances on a colossal scale. In particular for Möller's military play, *Der Graf von Walltron*, he had a camp with two hundred tents, troops on horseback and a real coach.

1782. In Pressburg his success did not last, and he closed his theatre and went to Vienna as guest artist at the Kärntnerthortheater.

1784. Schikaneder reopened his theatre at Pressburg, again with little success. The Emperor Joseph II visited the theatre and

---

[1] The material for this note has been taken principally from Komorzynski and Deutsch (*see* Bibliography).

was much impressed with the performance of a German comic opera.

1784–5. In Vienna Schikaneder had a successful season of German Singspiele under the patronage of Joseph II. (This was the Emperor, who, between the years 1778 and 1782, had himself attempted to establish a German theatre at the Court. Mozart's *Entführung aus dem Serail* was written for this theatre in 1782, but the opposition of the vested interests of the Italian court theatre was too strong even for the Emperor, and his German theatre idea came to an end in 1782.)

1785. Schikaneder separated from his wife. The latter started a new company with Friedel, an actor in her husband's company.

Schikaneder himself engaged as an actor at the National-theater in Vienna.

1786. Schikaneder successfully petitioned the Emperor for permission to build a new theatre in Vienna. For some unknown reason, however, Schikaneder did not avail himself of this opportunity, but instead formed another travelling company.

1787. Schikaneder and his company at Regensburg, under the official patronage of the Prince of Thurn and Taxis.

The repertory of the company at this time included Shakespeare's *Richard III*, Schiller's *Die Räuber, Kabale und Liebe* and *Don Carlos,* Lessing's *Emilia Galotti,* Mozart's *Entführung,* and Martin's *Cosa rara.* In addition, comic plays, comic operas, ballets, pantomimes and all kinds of fantastic entertainments devised by Schikaneder himself. A successful revival of *Der Graf von Walltron* in the open air led Schikaneder to write a similar military play based on *Walltron.* A third open-air spectacle, more ambitious even than these two, was performed on an island in the Danube. This play was a version of a Regensburg legend, worked up by Schikaneder into an enormous spectacle. Enthusiasm for fantastic open-air entertainments on a colossal scale became a mania with Schikaneder, and their popular success gave way to ironical comments from the critics about his bombastic schemes.

1789. Schikaneder and his company transferred to Vienna. There followed a reconciliation with his wife, and with her he became joint director of the "Theater im Starhembergischen

Freihause auf der Wieden." This was a wooden theatre, built, as its name implies, in the great courtyard of the house of the Starhemberg family outside Vienna. It had been taken over in 1788 by Friedel and Schikaneder's wife. Friedel left her, however, and died in 1789, and thus from his wife Schikaneder acquired the theatre with which his name is most often associated.

At this time the Italian opera again flourished at the Court, for the Emperor's attempt to establish a German court theatre had not been repeated. There was, however, an ever-increasing demand in Vienna for entertainments of a German nature, and this demand was principally met by Marinelli in his theatre in the Leopoldstadt. Marinelli's repertory consisted of innumerable versions of the "Kasperl" theme—that is, entertainments which continually reintroduced the same figure "Kasper," the type of the popular clown. In addition, there were magic plays, local Viennese pieces, and also many of Schikaneder's own comedies and Singspiele.

Schikaneder opened his new theatre in direct competition with Marinelli, freely copying the latter's ideas, and even devising a series of entertainments of the "Kasperl" type, with a new popular figure "Anton" as the hero. Schikaneder set out to study his Viennese public and to provide them with a repertory to suit their tastes. He drew upon his past experience and introduced spectacular shows, and also took from Marinelli the idea of magic entertainments. Whereas Marinelli catered primarily for the popular Viennese taste, Schikaneder, in addition to copying Marinelli in this respect, provided serious operas and plays. The first of these was *Oberon,* a magic opera by Giesecke, a member of his company, with music by Wranitzky. This opera was, in a sense, a forerunner of *Die Zauberflöte,* being written in the same style, and deriving its story from the same collection of fairy tales. For a second magic opera, *Der Stein der Weisen,* written by himself, Schikaneder commissioned several composers to write the music: Mozart contributed a duet.

At this time Schikaneder renewed his friendship of Salzburg with Mozart. Josefa Hofer, Mozart's sister-in-law, was a member of his company, and he joined the lodge of Freemasons to which Mozart also belonged. Probably the success of *Oberon* and of *Der Stein der Weisen* led Schikaneder to approach Mozart for a new magic opera on the same lines, knowing that he could rely upon Mozart's name to bring him a box-office success to help him out of his financial difficulties.

1791. *Die Zauberflöte* first produced. The enormous success of this work led to an enhancement of the serious element of Schikaneder's theatre, and it became a home of operas and concerts. Mozart's *Entführung, Figaro, Don Giovanni, Così fan Tutte* and *La Clemenza di Tito* were all performed, in addition to operas of Haydn and Benda, and others whose names are now forgotten. Concerts were frequent in the later years of the theatre's existence at which music of Mozart, Haydn and Beethoven and others were performed. On October 27th, 1798, Beethoven played one of his own pianoforte concertos in the theatre.

Besides these operas and concerts there were revivals of the military plays, and of plays by Lessing, Schiller and Shakespeare.

1791. Karl Mayer entered the lists in competition with Schikaneder and Marinelli with a popular German theatre in the Josephstadt.

Schikaneder continued with his company in the Freihaus-theater until 1801. During this time he experienced ups and downs, but he still could hold the Viennese public. He was essentially an adventurer, however, who spent money as fast as he made it, and in spite of the enormous success of many of his productions, always ended up in debt. In 1799 he found a rich merchant to back him, one Zitterbarth, who became joint director of the theatre, and undertook the financial responsibility. Thus in 1800, when Prince Starhemberg gave Schikaneder notice to discontinue his use of the wooden theatre, Zitterbarth bought a site and built the "Theater an der Wien" for him.

1801. This theatre, which was opened in 1801, incorporated all the latest and most up-to-date devices for scene shifting, and was described as the best-equipped theatre in Germany.

1802. In 1802 the first performance of *Die Zauberflöte* in the new theatre provided the opportunity for making full use of its machinery and equipment. This performance was also im-

APPENDIX

portant, because it established Schikaneder as the authoritative
"father" of the opera, as he called himself, and showed how the
opera should properly be produced. This was an answer to a
production of the work in a so-called new style which Braun had
given at the Kärntnerthortheater in 1801.

Schikaneder continued to direct the artistic life of the theatre
on and off until 1806, continuing with the same sort of repertory
as he had introduced in the old Freihaustheater. His methods
of staging, however, and particularly effects, introducing horses,
camels, etc., on the stage, gave the lead to other theatres
throughout Germany. He continued to produce new operas,
and several times approached Beethoven to compose one for the
theatre.

1804. Eventually Zitterbarth sold the theatre to Braun, the
director of the Hoftheater, who had been a bitter enemy of
Schikaneder. For fear of competition Braun had attempted to
prevent the building of the Theater an der Wien. When he
bought it, however, Braun was reluctantly compelled to engage
Schikaneder to direct the theatre in order to keep it alive. He
continued in this post until Braun resold the theatre in 1806.

1807—1809. Schikaneder became director of the town theatre in
Brünn. Here his mania for spectacular entertainments took
hold of him, and he introduced more and more fantastic
elements. He repeated his previous military plays on an even
more gigantic scale than before, and wrote a new one on a local
theme, *Die Schweden vor Brünn*. Eventually his plays became
nothing more than pageants and tableaux, and the public not
unnaturally lost interest.

1809. Schikaneder returned to Vienna, where he lived until he
died in 1812. His last years were passed in the utmost poverty,
relieved only by a grant for life from the director of his Theater
an der Wien of four per cent. of the takings of every performance of *Die Zauberflöte,* and by a benefit performance of his
Die Schweden vor Brünn by the members of the Leopoldstadt
theatre.

BIBLIOGRAPHY

(These books are referred to in the text by the names of the authors)

Bulthaupt, Heinrich. *Dramaturgie der Oper*. Leipzig: Breitkopf & Härtel, 1925.

Da Ponte, Lorenzo. *Memorie*. Bari: G. Laterza & figli, 1918. (Also available in English: *Memoirs of Lorenzo da Ponte*, translated by L. A. Sheppard. London: Routledge, 1929.)

Dent, Edward J. *Mozart's Operas; A critical study*. London: Chatto & Windus, 1913.

Dent, Edward J. *Don Giovanni*. English version. London: Oxford University Press, 1938.

Deutsch, O. E. *Das Freihaustheater auf der Wieden*. Vienna: Deutscher Verlag für Jugend und Volk, 1937.

Einstein, Alfred. "Concerning some Recitatives in *Don Giovanni*," *Music and Letters*, London, October 1938.

Hoffmann, E. T. A. *Don Juan*. Musicalische Novellen und Aufsätze. Leipzig: Insel Verlag.

Jahn, Otto. *Mozart*. New and enlarged edition by Hermann Abert. Leipzig: Breitkopf & Härtel, 1923.

Komorzynski, Egon von. *Emanuel Schikaneder*. Berlin: B. Behr's Verlag, 1901.

Lert, Ernst. *Mozart auf dem Theater*. Berlin: Schuster & Loeffler, 1921.

Rouché, Jacques. *La mise en scène de Don Juan*. Paris: Durand, 1934.

Schnerich, Alfred. *Wie sahen die ersten Vorstellungen von Mozart's Don Juan aus?* Zeitschrift der Internationalen Musikgesellschaft. Leipzig: Breitkopf & Härtel, January 1911.

Sonnleithner, Dr. Leopold von. *Don Giovanni. Wortgetreuer Abdruck des ersten italienischen Textbuches für Prag vom Jahre 1787, mit den für die Aufführung in Wien im Jahre 1788 getroffenen Abänderungen*. Leipzig: Breitkopf & Härtel, 1865.

Stefan, Paul. *Don Giovanni* and *Die Zauberflöte*. Vienna: Herbert Reichner Verlag, 1938.